What People about Martha

"Martha is one of the funniest writers alive today."

—Phyllis Diller, comedienne

"As nice as she is funny. And she is very nice."

—Jimmy Brogan, comedian and former head writer for *The Tonight Show* with Jay Leno

"Martha Bolton has an attitude that makes her writing special—she cares about her audience. That makes every reader part of her writing and makes it that much more enjoyable for anyone who reads or listens to any of her work."

—Gene Perret, Emmy Award winning writer of *The Carol Burnett Show*

"Few people can drive home a point with humor the way Martha can. She lives life in the laugh lane."

—Mark Lowry, comedian, singer, songwriter

"Martha Bolton brings her genius writing skills to express hard truths that we all need to chew on. Her unique gift of humor makes the going down so much sweeter."

—Kathy Troccoli, award-winning singer, author

"Martha makes you laugh the old-fashioned way—with her cleverness, wholesomeness, and realism."

—Ann Jillian, actress

"Martha Bolton is quickly becoming the Neil Simon of Christian drama."

—Bil Keane, "The Famil

"The best comedy writer I have ever worked with."

—J

If a Woman's Hair Is Her Glory, Why Am I Tweezing My Chin?

If a Woman's Hair Is Her Glory, Why Am I Tweezing My Chin?

Martha Bolton

Guideposts

New York, New York

If a Woman's Hair Is Her Glory, Why Am I Tweezing My Chin?

ISBN-13: 978-0-8249-4795-8

Published by Guideposts
16 East 34th Street
New York, New York 10016
www.guideposts.com

Distributed by Ideals Publications, a division of Guideposts
2636 Elm Hill Pike, Suite 120
Nashville, Tennessee 37214

Guideposts and *Ideals* are registered trademarks of Guideposts.

Acknowledgments

The following chapters originally appeared on newchristianvoices.com: "I Knew It All Along," "Up, Up and Away . . . But You're Going to Pay," "The Perfect Match," "Makin" Do," "The Upside of a Recession," "An Open Letter to the American Taxpayer," "Wisdom Comes with Age," "I Miss Landlines," "Bearing Gifts," "I Miss Christmas Carolers," "A Good Tradition," "A Cake of Fruit," "No Accident" and "Frost Warning."

Photograph of Diantha Ain on page 45 is courtesy of Diane Reichick; photograph of Mary Kolada Scott on page 169 is courtesy of Donald A. Scott.

Library of Congress Cataloging-in-Publication Data

Bolton, Martha, 1951–
    If a woman's hair is her glory, why am I tweezing my chin? / by Martha Bolton.
        p. cm.
ISBN 978-0-8249-4795-8
1. Aging–Humor. 2. Middle-aged women–Humor. I. Title.

PN6231.A43B654 2010
814'.54—dc22   2009033782

Cover design and illustration by Designworks
Interior design by Lorie Pagnozzi
Typeset by Aptara

Printed and bound in the United States of America
10 9 8 7 6 5 4 3 2 1

To My Grandchildren

KIANA, KYLE, KADIN, LILY, TRENT, LANCE AND CHASE—
THEY MAKE GETTING OLDER WORTH IT!

Contents

Part Four: We're a Force to Be Reckoned With

Part Five: It's All in How You Look at It

Part Six: A Few Minor Adjustments

Foreword

by Ann Jillian

"If it ain't on the page, it ain't on the stage!" is an adage long used in the entertainment industry. The written word profoundly affects every media. Whether it's in the stage, screen, radio or recording industry, the writer is essential. Those of us who have spent a large part of our lives working in these creative environments know the wisdom of this saying. As an actress, I understand the need for a well-written monologue, dialogue or joke. How sweet a feeling knowing your lines are effective in content and solid in structure before you even say them. Your personal delivery becomes the icing on the cake.

It takes a person with a number of creative talents to convey appropriate emotions. The writer is, at once, a dramatist and humorist, a psychologist and philosopher. A writer uses keen people-watching skills to build a realistic situation we can all recognize or even relate to. Then, in the case of a comedy skit, for example, the writer takes the acceptably realistic situation, reveals and stretches its absurdities, and makes us laugh heartily at our human foibles.

Our great comedians, throughout the years, either had all those talents to produce the desirable effects themselves, or appreciated the need to find witty minds that could supplement and finely tune their mischievous views of the world. In my career I had the opportunity to work with a number of notable names, among whom was a personal favorite of mine and someone I've had the pleasure of working with quite frequently, Mr. Bob Hope. Bob, whose outlook certainly spilled over the top with his own, certifiable talent, used writers to enhance and broaden his identifiably playful brand of humor. You know they had to be excellent; they had to stay on their toes to keep up with him. One of his writers was a woman, the *only* woman on his writing staff. Her name was Martha Bolton.

When I met Martha, I was interested to observe that she was not one of those new, tough women who had entered into a heretofore "man's world" . . . she stayed a "gentle-lady." She was neither from the old school nor from the new, off-the-wall types who were showing up more often on the sets of Hollywood. No, Martha was quite normal, which was refreshing. Her demeanor was quiet, but I soon found out we shared an appreciation of the absurd that had me guffawing several times, even before our first meeting was over. What a great sense of humor! No inappropriate jokes or language of any kind. Boy, this was great!

Then I found out that we had something else in common: our husbands were both sergeants from law enforcement. This last connection would prove to be handy years later for a movie in which I played a police detective, where I needed instruction in various techniques commonly used in the apprehension of a suspect. My husband Andy had served as one of Chicago's finest and gave me a few pointers, and Martha's husband Russ, one of LA's best, took me to the Los Angeles Police Academy, where I was given training in self-defense and tested in making correct and swift judgments with the use of a weapon in a life-sized simulation program. (Okay, a little over-the-top for a part in a television comedy movie—but nonetheless interesting). Martha and I spent professional and personal time together. We attended each other's important family celebrations. We had become friends.

As the years rolled on Martha would send me copies of the many books she wrote. What fun they were! I spent endless hours with a smile plastered across my face reading books with such titles as *I Think, Therefore I Have a Headache!*; *Growing Your Own Turtleneck . . . and Other Benefits of Aging*; *Didn't My Skin Used to Fit?*; *If Mr. Clean Calls, Tell Him I'm Not In . . . and Other Funny Stories from Family Life*; *Honey, the Carpet Needs Weeding Again!*; and *Who Put the Pizza in the VCR?* On a "comfy" note were *I Love You . . . Still*; *The Official Friends Book*; and *When the Going Gets Tough, the Tough Start Laughing.* I bought them for my friends as well. It was clear that Martha was a fine writer. She had—and still has—that distinctive ability to relate to, clarify and poke fun at our everyday joys, fears and annoyances. What is even more special is that she has the wonderful skill of weaving a sense of hope and optimism into her work. It is natural that I asked her to collaborate with me on a script I had in mind, one with a faith-filled message. I had an idea; she had the skills to make the idea live. It was a terrific experience. I wanted some of her sparkling humor in my special personal appearances because it always proved successful. Working with a fellow woman of faith is a pleasure. Knowing her is a treasure.

If you are reading Martha Bolton's work for the first time, be ready for a very pleasant experience. Sit back and get ready for a feel-good read from, as Bob Hope would put it, "a real nice gal."

Acknowledgments

Thank you to:

My husband, Russ, whom I have known since I was fifteen years old, and to whom I've been married since I was eighteen. He has been an integral part of my life for the greater part of it. I'm thankful for that.

My family that keeps growing year by year. I am blessed!

Good friends, old and new, who have given me plenty of laughs and memories along life's journey. Thank you for your faithful friendship.

Fellow Boomers that I have met over the years who share in this fun and amazing journey through the second half of life.

The editors at Guideposts who helped with the editing of this book.

And last but in no way least, you, the reader. We're all going through this aging process together. We need each other. And a good night cream. And a whole lot of laughs!

If a
Woman's Hair
Is Her Glory, Why Am
I Tweezing My Chin?

Introduction

If we're blessed enough to make it to the north side of fifty, it hardly seems fitting to complain. So we're not going to do that here. We are, however, going to take a lighthearted look at many of the changes that go along with this whole aging process. After all, continuing to collect birthdays still beats that other option.

If you don't mind, I've invited a few of my friends to share their over-fifty experiences too. You'll find these profiles sprinkled throughout the book. Like me (and I do hope you too), they're trying not to let the second half of life slip through their fingers. They're making new memories, seeing the world and having the time of their lives.

The over-fifty years are an interesting period. Changes—some welcome, some not—start happening to our careers, our attitudes, our priorities, and yes, our bodies too. Some of us retire, while some of us, as comedian George Burns would often joke, can't retire. "Who'd support my mom and dad?" he'd say.

So join me as we look at those things that middle-agers, for centuries, have had to deal with. We'll also cover challenges that are particular to middle-aged life today.

I hope by the time you reach the end of this book, you will have thought about what you want to accomplish, experience and discover in the second half of your life. If your priorities are a little out of whack, I hope you'll take the time to restructure them. If you've been spending too much of today fretting over tomorrow, I hope you'll learn to relax more and live in the now.

Most of all, I hope you'll realize the importance of fully appreciating every aspect of your life: the good, the bad, the ups and the downs, the laughter and the laugh lines. They're all a part of being alive.

Part One:

We Don't Mean to Complain, But. . .

I Knew It All Along

I KNEW IT. I KNEW IT, I knew it, I knew it. In fact, I've always known it was true, instinctively anyway, but it took a well-known personality to bring this truth to the attention of the American public. What is it that I know, and have known all these years? *Exercise can hurt you.* And television personality Matt Lauer has proved it.

Here's what happened. Apparently, Matt was out riding his bicycle one day. In other words, he was *exercising.* I'm sure he was feeling good about himself too. One mile, two miles; who knows how far he had gone? But then, right in the middle of all his peddling, all his sweating, all his bottled-water sipping, right in the middle of his *exercising*, what happens? A deer jumps out of nowhere right into his path. Matt was so startled that he got off his bike the hard way—flying over the handlebars and landing in a heap on the ground.

The accident dislocated his shoulder. *Did you get that?* He was exercising and his shoulder got dislocated.

So much for the misplaced guilt I've felt all these years for using my aerobics videos and DVDs as coasters.

Matt's shoulder and dignity have both mended now, but the simple truth remains: exercise may have some benefits, but it can also hurt you. Workout gurus and health club owners may try to convince us otherwise, but the evidence is too great to ignore.

Remember Olympic diver Greg Louganis? Remember when he hit the back of his head on that diving board? The world was watching, and the world let out a collective gasp. You know that had to hurt. And what was he doing when this unfortunate incident happened?

Exercising. And winning gold medals, but still . . .

Over the years, doctors, personal trainers, television talk-show hosts—they've all tried to shame us into exercising. They've told us that we should get up from our recliners and get moving. They've told us that exercise is good for our hearts, burns calories and keeps our muscles from atrophying. But who among them ever warned us that we needed to watch out for *deer*?

Poor Matt Lauer. He was caught completely off guard, as any of us would have been. If you sign up for water aerobics, you don't expect to have to watch out for crocodiles. If you step onto a tennis court to hit a few balls, the thought of a couple of wild boars showing up doesn't even cross your mind. And when you take a bike ride, you're not expecting Bambi to leap out of the bushes and try to jump on the back of your bike, especially when it's not a double-seater.

It wasn't Matt's fault.

I've distrusted exercise ever since my "unfortunate encounter" with a vibrating belt machine. It happened years ago when I tried using the machine to get rid of the cellulite on my arms. I leaned into the belt and let it shake one arm; then I let it shake the other arm. The following morning when I woke up and walked by the mirror, I discovered, to my shock and horror, that all of my upper-arm fat had slid down to my elbows. Now, as much as I like Popeye, that wasn't the look I was going for.

Nothing like that, or the deer or diving board incidents, ever happens in a recliner. I'll repeat that: *nothing like that happens in a recliner.*

Even Lance Armstrong fell off his bike during a race in Spain recently and broke his collarbone.

This is serious, folks. Exercise is dangerous! Sure, people who do it on a regular basis tend to look fitter, feel better and slide into their jeans a little easier than the rest of us. But let's not ignore the other reality here. Take a good hard look at those past photos of Matt in his shoulder sling, replay the Greg Louganis incident in your mind or (if you can handle it again) watch it on YouTube, or imagine my upper-arm fat resting on my elbows like two floaties, and then ask yourself: Is that the direction you really want to go?

I didn't think so.

AN OPEN LETTER TO DESIGNERS OF FASHION

Dear Sir or Madam,

First, allow me to take this opportunity to compliment you on your hard work and talents. You have done some amazing things with fabric, thread and accessories. Over the years, you've covered a multitude of all-you-can-eat sins with your creative use of cloth, and for that we thank you. You have shown us your latest creations on runways from Paris to New York, and we have been duly impressed. You have designed fashions for every stage of life—childhood, teens, twenties, thirties and now our more matronly years. You have offered style to each of us, from surfer gals to boardroom executives.

Lately, though, we have been noticing that you are spending a little more time on everyone else and less and less time on those of us of the Boomer generation. This seems a bit odd given the fact that Boomers are one of the largest growing segments of the apparel-buying public. Why, then, are you ignoring us?

When you do not provide fashions appropriate for our age group, you force us to shop in the younger generation's section of our local department store or boutique. Now as much as we like the idea of looking younger, short shirts—the kind that force our belly buttons to make a public appearance when they would much rather remain snugly behind one or two layers of cloth—do not please us.

We want to be fashionable. We want to be current. But what we do not want are clingy shirts that show off where our personal real estate has settled. Must you make shirts that are so tight, they show every lump and bump? Some of us would rather not have our ribbon candy waists accentuated in that way.

And please, can we quit skimping on the material? When it's hanging on the hanger, we shouldn't be able to see that much of the hanger. Unless, of course, the material is scratchy, in which case, go ahead and skimp. Most of us don't like scratchy. But since we are paying the prices you're charging for clothes these days, give us some material!

Sleeveless is fine for those of us who work out, like Michelle Obama. The rest of us, whose arm muscles seem to have loosened their grip and can whip around in the wind like a playing card in a bicycle spoke, would prefer longer sleeves.

Don't get us wrong, though. We don't want uninspiring styles, either. You may not realize this, but we Boomers can get quite discouraged by a trip to the mall. First, we often have to walk through the teen section, with their strobe lights flashing and their music blasting in our ears. Not only can that make our migraines explode, but we also have to admit there's an excitement and energy there that's not present in our section. Even the Career Woman section, with its business suits and air of chic sophistication, is often a far cry from what's waiting for us on our racks.

The formal-wear department (with all those gowns with side slits that seem to go up to the earlobe) doesn't help us, either.

By the time we reach our department, we're exhausted and we're depressed. We know it's our department because you've turned off all the music. The closest thing to anything melodic is the saleslady humming to herself as she hangs up next season's arrival of loose-fitting shirts and embroidered sweaters, which, come to think of it, look strikingly similar to last season's loose-fitting shirts and embroidered sweaters. And the season's before that.

So I ask you, fashion designers of the world, why would we want to buy more of the same? Never mind the fact that we do, I'm asking why you think we would want to? Give us variety. Give us something modest, but trendy. Give us a little attention. We want more than housedresses and loafers. We want to look as good as the twenty- and thirty-somethings; we just want to be comfortable at the same time. We don't want to be sentenced to spend the rest of our lives with a closet full of drab.

How about music in our department too? Tom Jones? Elvis? We can still move to the beat. You don't have to give us strobe lights, although a disco ball might be a nice touch.

As far as accessories go, could you do something about the weight of our earrings? Some women have been wearing large earrings all their lives and, well, not to state the obvious, their lobes are starting to droop from years of carrying around this excessive weight. No one warned us that this was even possible. Save us from ourselves!

Lastly, can we do something about our swimming-suit choices? No, really, *can we do something about our swimming-suit choices?* We're not playing tennis or ice skating, so why the little skirt? Don't get me wrong. We don't want the cutaway styles, either: those high-cut torsos that show more of the sides of us than our doctor has ever seen, hospital gowns notwithstanding.

I realize the cutaway bathing-suit style is supposed to give wearers the look of longer legs, but it is also the #1 cause of wedgies in this country, surpassing bullies two to one. We do not wish to support this.

Then there is the standard black swimsuit. We're tired of this too. Is black the only color you think we'd like? We stopped mourning our fortieth birthday years ago. We've accepted our age and now we're ready to party. *Give us some color!* We've grown into our skin. Okay, not really. Our skin has, for reasons unbeknownst to us, outgrown us. So that was a bad example. But my point remains, *we want color.*

I would like to thank you, though, for adding the slenderizing elastic in certain key areas. That was brilliant. In fact, you could add even more. Make the whole suit out of elastic; we won't care.

I realize this is America and you have a right to design whatever fashions you like. But we would appreciate it if you would start offering those of us over the age of fifty more of a choice. If you'll do this for us, we promise to wear your styles proudly. We'll tell all our friends who it is who designed the dresses, pantsuits, sportswear and formals we are wearing. We'll be loyal consumers of your fashion lines. Just listen to us. That's all we're asking. And an elongated, slenderizing fun-house mirror in the dressing room wouldn't hurt either.

Sincerely,
Americans against Fashion Discrimination

I Miss Not Knowing the Nutritional Value of My Food

WASN'T THERE ALREADY enough guilt in the world? We had our mothers, our teachers, our doctors and our mothers-in-law. Did we really need to add to the list of people who make us feel guilty?

Apparently, we did, because someone somewhere came up with the bright idea of putting a nutritional content chart on just about everything we eat now. Did we ask for this?

They did it—the enemy with the calorie counter. Couldn't they find something better to do with their time, like go out and get another round of Krispy Kremes?

Whatever happened to the guilt-free days of dunking your chocolate chip cookies into a glass of milk, without the cholesterol police showing up to haul you off to the bathroom scale for your trial and punishment?

Whatever happened to eating a burger without even thinking that it might contain some one thousand calories? We only cared if it contained cheese and a pickle (dairy and vegetable—two healthy food groups), and for that they condemn us.

Life was so much less stressful before nutritional value charts. We didn't have to worry about whether what we were eating would park itself in our arteries, causing a fork in the flow. Back then we could eat all the pork rinds we wanted, and never feel an ounce of shame. We could eat as many potato chips as we desired (of course, this was back when we could open the bag too). We didn't calculate how much fat was in the filling that we would lick from a certain famous chocolate cookie. We just opened the cookie, licked the filling from each cookie lid, and went on with our lives.

Those were the good old days; back before we were forced to admit that, yes, there might be some connection between what we eat and the condition of our bodies.

So whatever happened to those days? They're gone. And now the word is out that there is a price to pay for all those snacks. There has been one all along, but we were in denial. Denial tastes better than reality. And it's a lot less stressful way to live.

No matter how badly we'd like it to go away, though, nutritional labeling is no doubt here to stay. So the next time you're eating that chocolate bar, try not to look at the nutritional value while you're licking the wrapper. It'll only ruin your day.

Grandma Wars

ONE DAY WHILE I WAS EATING at a restaurant with my twin grandsons (1½ years old at the time), a lady at a nearby table struck up a conversation with me.

For obvious reasons, the conversation quickly turned to the subject of grandkids. Before I knew it, she had whipped out several photos of her six grandchildren. Overly proud grandparents can be pathetic, can't they? I had no choice but to meet her aggressive move head on. But not until she had brought out another whole stack of photos.

I told her how intelligent our twin grandsons were, and that they had a six-year-old sister who was a budding artist and . . . *oh, where were my pictures?* I quickly looked through my purse for some photos that I could present as evidence. Like all grandparents, I snap tons of pictures of my grandkids. But that day, I didn't have a single wallet-size or 4 × 6 on me.

The stranger saw my weakness and fired again with more pictures and stories of *her* grandchildren. She was beaming, triumphantly smiling that sort of Joker smile. She knew, or so she surmised, that the battle was over and the victory was hers.

Not so fast. When it comes to my grandkids, I don't throw up the white flag that quickly. I turned to my husband. Surely, Grandpa (or Pa-ka as the twins call him) would have some pictures in his wallet. I asked, but he didn't have any with him that day either. I turned to my daughter-in-law. She had to have a few photos. But she also was without ammunition.

My heart sank. Where were my back-up troops? This stranger had challenged me to a duel of grandchild photos (you may not be aware of this, but I'm pretty sure that's what the Andrew Jackson duel was over), and I had no weapon. I was doomed to go down in a blaze of defeat.

The stranger continued to hammer me with unfriendly fire. Another story of her grandchildren. Another photo. I tried to tell her about my other three grandchildren but couldn't get a word in edgewise. She was ruthless. She knew she had caught me by surprise, that I was ill-equipped and doomed to retreat in shame; and she was ruthlessly preparing to take full advantage of my weakness.

She went on and on extolling—and I'm sure exaggerating—the qualities of her grand-offspring, while I and the rest of our party were held prisoner. I'm not saying anything she did was illegal (although unfair flaunting of grandchildren in this way should be), but it was certainly an aggressive and cruel move on her part. Especially when my own grandchildren are clearly the best. (Not better than yours, I'm sure. Let's call that a tie. See, you're so much more reasonable than that lady was.)

What is it about grandchildren that make us think ours are the brightest, the handsomest, the prettiest, the kindest and the most talented in the world? Most of us didn't have this type of competitive spirit with our own kids. But grandkids bring out the General Patton in us. It's a fight to the finish.

It's almost like playing cards with your photographs.

"I see your photo album and raise you a wall portrait."

"I see your wall portrait and raise you a mural."

"I see your mural and raise you a home video of my granddaughter's preschool graduation."

"I see your home video and raise you a DVD of the football game where my grandson scored the winning touchdown."

"I see your DVD and raise you my granddaughter's diploma from Harvard."

"I see your Harvard diploma and raise you my grandson's military medals."

"I see your military medals and raise you my granddaughter's state basketball championship."

"I see your basketball championship and raise you my grandson's dental records. Not a single cavity in his whole mouth."

"I see those dental records and raise you my bumper sticker that says 'My grandson is an honor student.'"

"I see your bumper sticker and raise you the fact that my granddaughter is CEO of the company that makes that bumper sticker."

See what I mean? This kind of one-upmanship never ends well. It goes on and on, until one party has had enough and either surrenders or brings in the big guns. And I had certainly reached my limit that day. If she had taken out one more picture, I was going to have to fire back with everything I had. I was going to have to call someone to go by my house and get our digital photo display, the one that runs a slide show of some two thousand photos on a television-sized screen. This woman was going down.

She must have sensed the resurgence brewing, because she gathered up her photos, bid us good-bye, and retreated to her car. (I like to think of it as a surrender.)

Next time, though, I will not be caught unprepared. From now on, I'm going to start carrying my Power Point presentation with me everywhere I go. The projection screen might be cumbersome, but you do what you have to do.

AN OPEN LETTER TO SCAMMERS

Dear Sir or Madam,

No, I do not want to deposit your check for sixty-seven million dollars into my checking account. You will have to take care of that yourself. Besides, my deposit slip doesn't have room for that many zeroes.

No, I do not want to buy the side of beef you're selling out of the trunk of your car. I know you said you work at a restaurant and it's meat left over from a banquet, but I prefer buying my beef from someone who doesn't have an out-of-state license plate and a luggage rack full of suitcases.

No, I do not want to give you my address, my birth date and my Social Security number when you call me out of the blue and ask for them. You may be a very nice person with a warm and friendly voice, but you have no need for my personal information. If you are truly from my bank, or my credit card or insurance company, you would already have all of that information in my file.

No, I do not want to buy medicine from you, no matter how many e-mails you send me.

No, I do not want to send you money to buy a plane ticket to come to my country and marry me.

No, I do not need a new roof that I pay you for up front . . . only to never see you again.

No, I do not want to join in on your pyramid scheme.

No, I do not wish to call a phone number with a special area code that will route my call through Kenya.

No, I do not want to pay you money for a "prize" that I have won.

No, I do not want vacation property at the base of a volcano.

I do not want any of these things, so please quit sending me your e-mails and junk mail and stop calling me at all hours of the day and night. I'm not looking for a get-rich-quick scheme. Nor do I want anything enlarged on my body. I'm all for fishing but not phishing. I just want to be able to open my e-mail and not have the first twenty-six messages be from you. I don't want to nearly break my neck racing out of the shower to answer the phone and have it be you. I don't want to find your brochures and flyers in my mailbox. I'm sure it is profitable for you to do these kinds of things; otherwise, you'd move on to another line of work. But trust me, I am not a potential customer, so you can remove my address from your files. You are wasting your time and energy, as well as mine. If you don't understand me, let me put it another way:

Dear Sir or Madam, I am in most desperate need of your help. Leave me alone!

Sincerely,
A Bothered Boomer

I Miss Quiet Restrooms

REMEMBER WHEN public restrooms used to be quiet? You'd go in there and do whatever it was you went in there to do, and then you'd leave. No one thought they had to blast rock music in there, or jazz, or oldies but goodies. I even visited one Mexican restaurant recently that was piping in a Spanish lesson through the sound system.

Now, I ask you, are you comfortable with all of this noise at a time when you could use a little more quiet?

Some doctors' offices play loud music in their restrooms and then expect you to go in there and leave them a sample. How do you do that when you have a front-row seat, so to speak, to a Bruce Springsteen concert? Whenever I'm in that situation, I have to sit through half the CD before I finally just give up. It's only a simple fact of life: If the music doesn't go, we won't either.

Another loud noise that has encroached upon our peace in public restrooms is the hand dryer. It's always been loud, but now they've put in those high-powered machines that'll suck the freckles right off of you. Was that really necessary?

As if that wasn't bad enough, they've also put in faucets that turn on all by themselves. You could be the only one in the restroom and suddenly a faucet goes on. And then another. And another. It would be relaxing, sort of like listening to a waterfall CD, if the flood waters weren't starting to seep under the door into your stall.

The worst noise, though, has to be the sound of people talking on their cell phones. Is this really a place to conduct your personal business? Of course not. Look around. Do you see a fax machine in here? A desk? It's not an office. It's a "rest" room. Let the rest of us rest in peace.

Yes, I liked it a lot better when restrooms were quiet. Without the rock concert, without the dryer and without the flush that sounds like a 747 taking off underneath you. I miss that quiet. You probably do too.

PROFILE: MARGARET BROWNLEY

Author of *A Lady Like Sarah*

Age: Old enough to know better

Margaret on an Alaskan glacier

What is the most outrageous thing you've done since passing your fiftieth birthday?

I don't think most people would consider this outrageous, but my answer is: zipline through the Costa Rica forest. I also sat on Fabio's lap (yep, the "I can't believe it's not butter" guy) and helped judge a romance book cover-model contest.

Is there anything you haven't done that you would still like to do?

Zipline through the Costa Rica forest with my eyes open (ha, ha). I've been to all fifty states, and I'd like to do more traveling.

But with the world the way it is, who knows? And of course, I still have about a hundred books I want to write.

What do you think is the single best thing about growing older?

The freedom of doing what you want without worrying about what others think. It's also fun to see the fruits of your labor. Watching my children become adults and build their families has been a joy. Raising children is the only job where you have to wait thirty years to find out if you blew it. (I also found out that older folks are the first ones released during a hostage takeover. That's nothing to sneeze at.)

Name one thing that you appreciate more with age.

Life, health, family, friends and a good bra. Seriously, I think it's the ability to know what's important and what's not. I think the name for this is wisdom.

What would you say to those who have just reached or will soon reach retirement age?

Don't retire, regroup. Find something you love to do and go for it. I see too many people fade away when they retire. Nothing keeps us feeling and acting young quite like passion. Find something you're passionate about and then do it.

Looking back on your life, what's the most important thing you have learned?

I've learned how short life is and how fast children grow up. I've learned that nobody cares if the wash is stacked up or the bed is unmade. I've learned that nobody dies if you miss a deadline. I've learned to laugh at rejection and celebrate every little success. I've learned you should cherish the people with you today because no one knows what tomorrow will bring.

Part Two:

If You Don't Do It, Who Will?

Ten Serious Questions
I Ponder Late at Night
between Leg Cramps

SO THERE I WAS AGAIN, lying in my bed pondering ten serious questions—the great mysteries of the universe, of course—when the thought suddenly occurred to me that maybe you spend your evenings asking yourself such questions too. I wouldn't be surprised. We have to do something in the lull between leg cramps, right?

If any of the following questions bothers you, too, feel free to ponder them along with me:

1. If I'm going to dance every night to the beat of my leg cramps, why don't I at least turn on some music?
2. Where did my eyebrows go, and why did they leave without saying good-bye?
3. Why is my elbow skin starting to pool?
4. Who's been coming into my bedroom in the middle of the night and painting all these funny little brown spots on me? Why don't they leave me alone? I was fine with freckles.

5. Whenever I sit down to eat, why does so little fill me up these days? I'm so confused about this phenomenon that I have to repeat the process seven or eight times throughout the day just to believe it.

6. When did I grow my own belly purse, and why isn't there a pocket on it that I can use?

7. If I'm twenty pounds heavier than I was ten years ago, where did all this extra skin come from and why am I not filling it out?

8. What's with the puffiness under my eyes? I don't remember ordering this, and if I did, can I return it?

9. Why do my knees buckle without warning, forcing me to curtsy when I'm not even meeting the Queen?

10. If a woman's hair is her glory, why am I tweezing my chin?

Watching Out for Each Other

WHY IS IT THAT the older we get, the more medications we have to remember to take? The opposite should be true. They should have given us all these things to remember when we were young and could easily recall them.

In our youth, the only pill most of us had to remember to take was a vitamin. But once menopause and man-o-pause set in, someone started prescribing all sorts of medication for us, each with its own set of instructions.

"Take this three times a day with food."

"Take this four times a day on an empty stomach."

"Take this twice a day, and avoid exposure to the sun."

"Replace this medicated patch once a month."

"Take one pill now, two tomorrow and three the following day, increasing one pill per day until supply is gone."

"Take four pills today, three tomorrow and continue to decrease one pill daily until symptoms subside, or your pharmacist's house is paid off, whichever comes first."

"I don't care when you take this pill."

How are we supposed to remember all of these instructions?

My father's list of medications seemed to grow with each birthday. He finally had so many prescriptions to take that he would arrange the day's worth of pills on a plate, and then turn the plate as he worked his way through the doses throughout the day. Once the plate had gone full circle and was empty, the entire process would begin all over again the following day.

My mother, who battled lymphoma in the final chapter of her life, had a chart to help her remember when to take all of her medications. That made keeping track a little easier.

Whatever system you use to remember your prescriptions—a chart, a pill box, a dinner plate, a tattoo—the important thing is to not accidentally double up on your medications. This can be serious.

My husband and I aren't really into tattooing our bodies with our medication needs, but we do realize the importance of keeping a chart of some sort. Depending on each other to remember who's taken what medicine isn't working anymore. Especially on those occasions when neither one of us can remember.

Did I take my medicine?

Yeah. I think you did.

I don't think I did.

Okay, maybe you didn't.

Don't agree with me if you don't really know.

Well, I thought you took it, but I could be wrong.

But you could be right. If you think you remember my taking it, maybe I took it.

Then maybe you took it.

I don't think I took it.

Now that I think about it, I think you're right. I don't think you took it, either.

Are you just saying that because you want to get back to your TV show?

No. I really don't think you took it. Now give me back the remote.

Well, then, maybe I should go ahead and take it.

Good. The remote . . . ?

But what if I did take it? I don't want to overdose.

Then don't take it.

How sure are you that I didn't take it?

Not as sure as I am about wanting the remote.

So you're not a hundred percent in agreement that I didn't take it?

Look, I don't think you took it. But I could be wrong. That's all I can say.

Okay. I'll take it now then.

Good . . . now give me the. . . . Oh, no, wait. Don't take it. I remember now. You did take it.

(Spewing the pill across the room) Are you sure?

Yep, we were in the kitchen, the phone rang, and you asked me to answer it because you were in the middle of taking your medicine.

Oh, yes, I remember now. You're right. I did take it. Right after I took my Ginseng. . . . I did remember to take my Ginseng, didn't I?

I don't know. I'm not sure. Did I remember to take mine?

Oh, well, let's skip it today. So who was that phone call from anyway?

Phone call? What phone call?

Maybe a medical chart tattoo isn't such a bad idea after all.

Just for Clarification

AS WE GET OLDER, many of us tend to do more rationalizing than we used to. This is especially true in the area of exercise. Often, what we now count as "exercise" would hardly resemble exercise to anyone else, yet we still convince ourselves (and try to convince our doctor) that our feeble attempts at "moving" should count.

So this baby boomer brand of rationalization doesn't start happening to you, I have provided the following tips:

- Typing e-mails to the beat of a "Sweating to the Oldies" DVD does not count as exercise.

- Swatting a fly over your head is not considered a jumping jack. (But nice try.)

- Lying face down on your pillow for a nap cannot be counted as half a push-up.

- Submersing yourself in your bathtub is not the same as swimming a lap, no matter how much splashing you do.

- Peeking over the fence to spy on your neighbors is not a chin-up.

- A lazy river inner-tube is not considered workout gear.

- Bending down to get the Ben and Jerry's out of the freezer is not a squat. Well, it is, technically, but it won't burn a lot of calories . . . unless you keep going back for more.
- Reaching for a plate of brownies does not count as a crunch, no matter how far away the brownies are.
- Accidentally tumbling down a flight of stairs is not even in the same category as gymnastics.
- Putting on a girdle with metal stays should not be considered pressing iron.

Getting Tough on Stuff

IN THESE DIFFICULT TIMES, people are trying to supplement their income any way they can. One way some people get a little extra cash is by selling off some of their prized possessions. I hope that they're not selling things that they're going to regret later. But if the items they're selling have been cluttering up their home for years, not being utilized or appreciated, or for that matter even taken down off the shelf or out of the closet and looked at, and if the items hold little, if any, sentimental value, maybe they have the right idea.

We all might be surprised to learn that those prized "antiques" we've hung onto all these years aren't worth as much as we thought they were.

"Hey, looky here. Grandpa's old violin. Elwood, check and see if it says 'Stradivarius' over there next to the Walmart label."

We might have to admit that the paint-by-numbers portrait we picked up from a garage sale twenty years ago isn't a long-lost Van Gogh after all, even though the paint-by-numbers imprint on the back does appear to be in French.

That vase we picked up at the Dollar Store three Christmases ago isn't from the Ming Dynasty either.

Maybe our hesitation to part with some of the stuff we've collected over the years has a lot to do with how many episodes of *Antiques Roadshow* we've watched lately.

But just as it's healthy to clear out your closets of the clothes you are no longer wearing, there's something freeing about getting rid of the clutter around your house too. The "stuff" that George Carlin used to talk about.

When I leave this world, I don't want my family to have to climb over a bunch of boxes of stuff to find me.

An elderly friend became seriously ill and an ambulance had to be called to take her to the hospital. The EMTs who arrived on the scene weren't able to get the stretcher down the hall to this woman's bedroom because of all the boxes of papers, books and . . . well, stuff. The only way they could get her out of the house was to lift her out through her bedroom window, maneuver her onto the gurney, and then wheel her around the house and into the waiting ambulance.

On hearing her retell her adventure a few days later when I visited her at the hospital, we both couldn't help but break into a fit of laughter. She had an amazing, let-it-all-hang-out wit, and her description of the ordeal was nothing short of hysterical. To add insult to injury, on her way out of the window, her gown kept slipping off her shoulder, revealing much more than she wanted to. Her "preponderances were showing" was how she so delicately put it.

I want to make sure I don't ever end up in my friend's situation. I want to sort through my piles of paper and boxes now before things get to that level. I want to get rid of whatever isn't of value (sentimental or otherwise) to anyone.

I want to. And I'm going to. I really am. No, really, I am. Soon. Really soon. It's either that or I'm going to start sleeping a lot closer to the front door.

Helmets

THE OTHER DAY as my husband and I were watching television, a commercial came on advertising walk-in bathtubs. Bringing a handful of popcorn to his mouth, he paused and said, "We ought to look into one of those."

Considering the fact that he is a shower person and I am a bath person, I could only assume that his suggestion was directed toward me.

Now, I have nothing against the product. In fact, I'm sure it fills a need for thousands of people. But I can still climb in and out of a bathtub on my own, thank you very much (provided no one has spilled shampoo in there, and provided there's a rail, and provided . . . well, you get the idea).

I can't fault him, though, for suggesting it. He thought he was being helpful. As we get older, falling and breaking a hip is serious business. When my grandmother broke her hip, it was the beginning of the end for her, especially once a staph infection set in soon afterward. So when the time comes, I'll probably consider a product like a walk-in bathtub. But I don't think we're there yet.

What I could use in the meantime, though, is a helmet. Not for the bathtub, although that might not be a bad idea either. But a helmet for use throughout my day. I can't tell you how many low-hanging ceiling fans I have run into, not to mention all the open cupboard doors that I've hit with the top of my head. Don't you hate that? You're looking for something in a lower cupboard, and then you stand up and *whack!* I wonder why that kind of injury has never been covered on *E.R.* or one of the other doctor shows. Maybe the bloodcurdling screams would be too graphic even for television.

There are other head injuries I have to watch out for. Such as bonking heads with my two-year-old twin grandsons when they run toward me and forget to stop. All three of us could probably use helmets for that.

Maybe I should just go ahead and get full-body armor. I wouldn't wear it twenty-four/seven, but there are times throughout my day when I could see a metal suit coming in handy. I have a tendency to walk into things. I've walked into poles at the mall. (I still say someone moved them when I wasn't looking. Probably the same person who sneaks in and moves the stores around. Have you noticed this? It's hard to catch them in the act because they do it so quickly. You might be in a store only five minutes, but by the time you walk out, the other stores are all in different places.)

"Hey, what happened to Sears? It was right here a minute ago."

"Are you sure?"

"Of course, I'm sure. I'm telling you, it was right here. It was right next to the pet shop that's over . . . hey, where'd the pet shop go?"

What kind of sick person gets their enjoyment out of moving stores around like this? They need help.

Of course, once you look at the directory, you realize that both Sears *and* the pet shop are exactly where they're supposed to be . . . at another mall. Why someone hasn't come out with a Mall GPS before now is beyond me.

But back to the furniture.

I've walked into coffee tables and sofas, breaking both of my baby toes several times each (you know, the two toes that go "Ow! Ow! Owww!" all the way home.) A few years ago I even broke the big toe on my right foot when I missed a step on my front porch. (Just in case you're wondering, I've never had a drink of alcohol in my life.)

You know, now that I've given it a little more thought, maybe a walk-in bathtub isn't such a bad idea after all. Or better yet, why doesn't someone invent a drive-through bathtub? Then we'd have a seatbelt to protect us too. And just think what it would save us on car washes.

Hmm . . . I might just be on to something there.

Last in Line

LIKE MANY WOMEN, I have a tendency to put myself last. Some might say this is a good quality. Good or not, I have it, others know I have it, and no matter what I do to change it, it's what feels most natural to me.

My mother had this quality. When she died, she had only a handful of dresses hanging in her closet. She wore the same pair of sandals for years. She wouldn't get rid of a purse until the strap broke from the weight of all the items she carried in it. Clothes and accessories weren't a priority for her.

Even in her own house, she didn't take the master bedroom. She took one of the smaller ones upstairs.

If you look up sacrificial love in any book on human behavior, you would find not only my mother's picture but also a message from her asking if you've eaten.

At holiday meals, she'd be the last person to sit down and eat. Even though we'd try to get her to sit down, she always found just "one more thing" that she thought needed taking care of. By the time she sat down, her plate of food was usually cold, but I never heard her complain.

When she was diagnosed with lymphoma at seventy-two years of age, it took a lot of convincing to get her to take time off from her job and take care of herself for a change. She wasn't used to it. Like the Energizer bunny, she was programmed to keep going and going and going.

But eventually, even the Energizer bunny needs to be recharged. Sadly, and much too soon, the end came one day.

I wish my mother had taken better care of herself. I wish she had shared the dizziness she was feeling at work. I didn't see it until we took her to Disneyland for her seventy-second birthday and noticed that she had to stop and rest between rides.

The next day I made an appointment with a doctor, in spite of her protests. I thought it might have been her heart. I never dreamed it was cancer.

I wish my mother wouldn't have pretended that she was invincible. She wasn't. And I miss her.

My mother's behavior has affected how I treat myself. I don't always share when I'm sick, sad, hurt or fearful either. Like my mother, I sometimes think I'm invincible.

Maybe you do too.

We're not.

Certainly, some people are more than willing to divulge every ache and pain they've ever had. Some even crave the attention that sickness brings so much so that they'll fabricate their symptoms or circumstances. Such a need can be a bottomless pit of misery that only years of counseling will help.

But most of us do our best to stay out of hospitals. We eat those apples every day to "keep the doctor away." We don't want to be sick. And when we do get sick, we might mention it in passing, but it certainly isn't our focus.

I've been diabetic for over thirty-eight years, but I refuse to let the disease define me. By now, I have had some thirty-nine thousand injections. You can't really see all those holes, but if you stand too close to me while I'm drinking a glass of water, you're likely to get a shower.

I take my medicine and do what I can to stay healthy, but otherwise I try to look at my circumstances with a healthy dose of humor.

That doesn't mean, though, that I can't let friends and family help. We are made for community, so not letting someone else share in our challenges isn't always a good quality.

If we don't reach out when we're hurting, how will we ever know that people care? How much depression could be avoided if people would only speak up and let someone, at least a few close friends or family members, know the depth of their despair? Sure, some people might not show much concern, even after you tell them your pain. But you're better off to find that out about them now and realize they're not your source for help and encouragement so you can move on and find a better support system.

So don't stay in the back of the line, keeping all your needs to yourself. Speak up. Most people would be eager to offer their love and support . . . if only they knew you needed it.

When I Am Old, I Shall Wear Jewelry

I DON'T WEAR a lot of jewelry. I never have. Other than my wedding ring and a necklace on which hangs two police badges my husband gave me, a "Mom" charm my son gave me, and my birthstone that my sister gave me, I don't wear much in the way of jewelry.

I'm afraid of losing the set of pearls and an engraved diamond watch that my husband gave me, so I hardly ever wear them. Before you judge me, know that it is with good reason that I'm overly cautious. The three-pearl ring he gave me in high school surfaced recently, and I was so excited about finding it that I immediately put it on my finger and wore it to the store. It wasn't a very good fit (I guess my fingers have lost some weight over the years—only my fingers), and the ring apparently slipped off. I didn't even realize it was missing until I got home. I called the store to see if anyone had turned it in, and even searched my car several times, but both of those efforts were dead ends.

I was luckier when I lost my wedding ring. It fell off my finger once while I was standing nearly waist deep in murky lake water. I felt it slip off, and both my heart and the ring immediately sank.

My husband and sons took turns diving down into the water, trying to find it. After about an hour of searching the bottom of the swimming area, just as it was starting to get dark, just when we were about to give up, I found it.

So, you see, this is precisely why I prefer to leave my good pieces safe at home in my jewelry case.

The other day, though, as I was going through my jewelry box, I had a change of heart. I thought to myself, *What am I waiting for?* I've held onto some of this jewelry for years, even decades. Sure, it's all still here, safe and sound, but what good is it doing anyone?

The hard truth is this—I'm living in the last half of my life. So why am I denying myself this simple pleasure? As long as it's not my wedding ring that gets lost again, I can handle it. And even if I do lose my wedding ring again, we could get another one. It's not a life-or-death issue.

I wouldn't have any of this jewelry had it not been a gift or had I not wanted it enough to buy it in the first place. So why am I not making some memories with the jewelry, especially those pieces that were gifts?

Nothing is sadder than to take inventory of all the things we've hung onto for years—things we've carted from house to house when we've moved—only to realize that we haven't made a single personal memory that connects us to any of it. I have purses I've never used, dresses I've never worn, jeans I've never been skinny enough to get one leg in, and jewelry that just sits there collecting dust.

Life is too short not to enjoy the things around us, especially those things that are already bought and paid for. So if you, too, have something just sitting there getting dustier and dustier, or hanging in your closet getting hanger creases, take it out and put it on. Vow not to leave anything behind that can be advertised at your estate sale as "never been used."

PROFILE: DIANTHA AIN

Actress, poet, artist, songwriter, playwright
Age: 80

What is the most outrageous thing you've done since passing your fiftieth birthday?

I signed up for a writing course, entered contests and won awards for poetry, writing and music. I wrote and illustrated a poetry book, which led me to the most rewarding work I've ever done, cultivating creativity in children.

Writing haiku, a Japanese form of poetry, is another peak on my creative graph. I created a hundred different greeting cards, wrote more than four hundred poems for a grief-book project, "Grieving God's Way," and was the haiku editor for *Bereavement Magazine* for five years.

Is there anything you haven't done that you would still like to do?

The one thing I would still like to do is finish a collection of poetry and prose capturing my childhood memories from when I lived in Colonia, New Jersey, in the 1930s.

What do you think is the single best thing about growing older?

Probably the single best thing about growing older is becoming a grandmother and then a great-grandmother. My special bonus was having both a grandchild and a great-grandchild named after me. I am Diantha IV, descended in a family chain from 1778. So now we have V and VI.

Name one thing that you appreciate more with age.

The one thing I appreciate most with age is my creative ability. When I was young, I presumed that anyone could do anything I could do. I'm older and wiser now. I thank God on a regular basis for the talents He has bestowed upon me, and it fosters a strong obligation in me to use them wisely.

What would you say to those who have just reached or will soon reach retirement age?

To people who are retiring, I would say, "Turn your dreams to realities while you can, and be sure you've got your priorities in the right order."

Looking back on your life, what's the most important thing you have learned?

Looking back, the most important thing I've learned is not to judge myself by anyone else's standards. Each one of us is unique and different. A two-sided mug in my collection says it best. "Success is loving what you do/ Success is doing what you love." I think that's my philosophy now.

Part Three:

Who Moved My Bran Muffin?

I Miss In-Store Coffee Shops

IF YOU WERE LUCKY enough to live near a Woolworth's or a Thrifty's Drugstore that also had a coffee shop, you were a lucky person indeed. Remember those wonderful in-store coffee shops? They were great, weren't they? And so handy. If you happened to get hungry during your shopping spree, all you had to do was walk over to the counter and order a sandwich. Or a Swiss steak dinner. Or some hot apple cobbler with vanilla sauce and ice cream.

Not very many stores have their own cafeterias anymore. They were replaced by mall food courts. But that's not the same. In-store cafeterias had booths, and stools where you could sit at the counter. The cook and the wait staff often knew you on a first name basis. They didn't even have to ask you what you wanted; they knew your usual order.

The best place to sit at an old-fashioned in-store diner was the counter. There you could rub elbows (literally) with other locals and share your opinions about the day's news. It was hometown social life and it didn't get any better than that.

My favorite items on the menu were the above-mentioned Swiss steak and the hot apple cobbler. No meal before or since can compare. They were the best. And the whole meal, including dessert, cost less than two bucks. Maybe that's the main reason I miss the in-store diner so much: the prices. Just thinking about what two dollars could buy you back then brings tears to my eyes. Nowadays, some restaurants microwave a composition meat product, ladle some canned gravy on top of it, plop it down next to a grayish-white mountain of instant mashed potatoes and a sliver of a green bean or two, and for that they charge you nine bucks.

One of the best things about the in-store diner was watching the cook. Those short-order cooks could put on a perfectly choreographed show that would rival a New York City ballet . . . only with a lot more grease.

We may not have supported the in-store diners like we should have (maybe that's why so many of them closed up shop), but when we did eat there, we certainly got our money's worth. These days, we eat while we shop, only we do it in front of the television set or the computer. It's just not the same.

I miss that Friday Swiss steak special, topped off with hot apple cobbler. But I still have my memories. And they don't have nearly as many calories.

A New Wardrobe

LATELY, I'VE BEEN giving away my clothes. Not the ones I'm wearing, of course, but the ones that have started bulging their way out of my closet and drawer space.

It's amazing how many pieces of clothing we can collect over a lifetime, isn't it? We hang on to styles that have long since become passé. We refuse to let go of clothes that no longer fit us or are in disrepair. We have jeans that won't zip, shirts that don't button, and backless shoes that didn't start out that way.

We don't take the time to fix them and we never wear them; yet they remain in our closets. *Why?*

Good question.

The main reason I've hung on to my old clothes is that whenever I decide to clean out my closet, I'm not in the right mood for the task. Cleaning closets requires the appropriate mind-set. You can't be in a nostalgic mood when you do it, because then you won't be able to part with a single item. Each piece of clothing will have a memory, or it will hold the hope that someday you're going to get to wear it again. After all, don't all styles make a comeback eventually? Bell-bottoms did. And paisley shirts. So, of course, parachute pants are next in line, right?

Never try to clean out your closet in the winter, either. In the winter you're cold and will therefore want to hang on to everything, just in case a blizzard hits and you lose the power in your home. Visions of your house buried in some twelve feet of snow, even though you live in Florida, will keep you from letting go of anything that can potentially keep you warm. Who knows? You may have to layer yourself with five or six of those sweaters that you were wanting to give away, just to keep from freezing to death.

On the other hand, in the hot and humid months of summer, giving away your clothes is easy. Walk into your closet when the temperature is over one hundred degrees and everything will look hot and scratchy to you, I guarantee it. You won't be able to give the clothes away fast enough. You may have loved that cute, fluffy sweater in the spring, but if it's hanging there in the summer, rubbing up against your arms every time you move a hanger, you're going to want to toss it.

I'm telling you—this is the perfect mood and season to go through your closet. You'll give everything away, including your husband's and children's clothes, barely remembering to remove your loved ones first before dropping the items off at a local charity or consignment store.

Another problem I have with clearing out my closet is knowing when a style is out of date. If the outfit still has some wear left in it, I feel I should hang on to it. That's why some of you may have seen my husband and me dressing like *That '70s Show* from time to time. If the fabric isn't threadbare, I tend to hang on to it.

It would help if fashions came with a freshness date, like meat and dairy products. Then the fashionably challenged among us (ahem) would know when it's time to get rid of certain clothes. My main problem is that it takes me a while to get brave enough to venture into any out-of-the-norm styles. By the time I finally try out a new fashion trend, it's about two seasons out of vogue.

A fashion freshness date would, therefore, be a tremendous help. I'm tired of putting on outfits and having some well-intentioned friend or stranger say to me, "Oh, that's so nineties," or "Puh-lease, you're not seriously going to wear that, are you?"

I usually laugh and pretend I merely put the outfit on as a joke. But when I'm already at the event, that excuse doesn't play so well.

Because clothes don't have a freshness date, I'm left to make my fashion decisions on my own. Or by looking through magazines. This works, but not if the magazines are ten years old, which most of mine are. *Hmm*, maybe that's my problem.

As soon as I cart off all my hot, unwanted clothes, I usually find myself being amazed at two things: how big my closet has suddenly become and how many more outfits I have just discovered. There will be clothes hanging in there that I had forgotten all about owning, and you won't believe how many brand-new combinations I find—outfits that I had never even thought about putting together.

If the years have shown us anything, they've shown us that our minds can be a lot like closets. We keep a lot of out-of-date things in there too—things that we should have long since discarded. Situations that remain in disrepair, and unhappy memories that passed their freshness date a long time ago.

But we have to be in the right mood for this kind of cleaning too. We have to quit thinking that wrapping ourselves in the warmth of familiar hurts will insulate us from the next crisis, which may or may not ever come. Instead, we should wait for that one sunshiny day when we're tired of dealing with matters of the past. Then, we'll be motivated to finally clear it all out—not denying its existence but simply refusing to let it crowd out our future. When we do, we'll no doubt be amazed at how many good things had been hanging there all along, hidden in the bulging clutter of our memories, waiting to be rediscovered and appreciated.

AN OPEN LETTER TO BUFFET OWNERS

Dear Sir or Madam,

I am writing to thank you from the bottom of my heart for the service that you faithfully continue to provide to the American public, especially those of us over the age of fifty. Before you came into our lives, we were doomed to eat only one plate of food, and in our naive state, we thought that was enough.

But you have changed all that. We now know that most of us can easily polish off three plates or more and have enough room left for dessert. We want to thank you for opening up our minds (and our belts) to this fact.

We do have a question, however. It is simply this: How do you do it? How do you serve all of us as much as we can possibly eat and still make a profit? It doesn't make mathematical sense. I've personally witnessed some of the plates that your faithful patrons have piled up, and by my estimations, they would put any restaurant in the red. We could hold the Winter Olympics on some of those mountain peaks of mashed potatoes. And that's not even counting the piles of roast beef, chicken and sometimes even prime rib. True, you serve a lot of pasta dishes, and you bring out the dinner rolls at regular intervals to fill us up; but still. You have to be operating at a loss.

When it comes to people making a sacrifice for our country, you are right there with the rest of our nation's heroes.

Yet when is the last time anyone honored *you*? When was the last time your patrons put down their forks, rose up to their feet, and applauded your generous and tireless efforts? When was the last time you were cheered for simply bringing out more seafood salad and barbequed chicken wings?

I have a feeling that the answer is never.

Well, I, for one, believe it is high time we changed all that. It's time you received your long overdue praise. That is why I am writing this open letter to each and every one of you.

On behalf of the American public, I want to thank you first and foremost for even giving us the option of eating all we can. You have unselfishly given us true value for our dollar, and in this economy, we sincerely appreciate that.

We also want to thank you for the dignity with which you have treated us. When we're standing at the serving trough, piling our plates up to the ozone layer, you never embarrass us by saying such things as "You gonna eat all that?" or "You know, you can get a second plate."

You simply watch us walk by, balancing one plate in our left hand, a second plate in our right hand, a dessert cup tucked in the fold of our elbow, and a dinner roll between our teeth, and you never say a single discouraging word to us. We thank you for this. We know we are eating far more than our diets call for (the average buffet eater consumes about a week's worth of calories in one sitting), but you never infringe on our joy by pointing this out to us. You, sir or madam, are a saint. God bless you for the roll, I mean role, you have played in the contentment of so many. There is no better feeling than to get three or four plates of food for the price of one. Life does not get much better than that. Never mind that our blood sugar rushes to pre-coma levels; you make us very, very happy, and for that we will be forever indebted to you.

Now get out of our way. We're going back for more!

Most gratefully,
Buffet Fans of America

I Miss the Milkman

REMEMBER THE MILKMAN? That guy who would deliver fresh milk, eggs and even a loaf of bread to our doorsteps in the wee hours of the morning?

My family had a milkman when I was growing up. I remember being awakened by the sound of his truck pulling up out front. Then I'd hear him open his door and walk to the rear of his vehicle. This was followed by the unforgettable sound of glass bottles hitting together in the metal carrier as he delivered our order to our front porch.

When the sun came up, I'd rush to open the door to see what he had left. If a bottle of chocolate milk was sitting there, it felt like Christmas morning all over again.

I continued the practice of at-home milk delivery when my own sons were small, but I wouldn't just order milk and chocolate milk. I'd order eggs, English muffins and, on some mornings, even bacon. (We lived in Southern California at the time, and in the summer months if I didn't get the bacon inside before the sun was too high in the sky, it would practically start sizzling.)

Having a milkman was like having your own personal shopper. Of course, when the monthly bill came, you had to take a second loan out on your house just to pay him. But it was wonderfully convenient.

The milkman had to start work early to get all of his morning deliveries done. I'm sure he and the paperboy crossed paths on many occasions; there's no telling how many times the milkman took a hit to the back of the head by the *New York Times*, all in the name of service.

We owe a lot to the milkman. That's how many of us got our daily supply of calcium. And many milkmen even gave their customers an interest-free line of credit. When we were between paychecks, our milkman was more than happy to leave us the milk and bill us later. He, and other businesses like him, never would have dreamed of charging twenty-four percent interest or making their customers fill out three-page credit applications. They just trusted you for it. After all, they knew where you lived.

When business slowed down, the milkman didn't ask for a bailout, either. He just parked his truck and disappeared into the cloud of dust caused by the minimarkets and all-night grocery stores that were being built all over the country. A few milkmen may still be in operation today, still getting up in the middle of the night to deliver their bottles of milk and other dairy products. And I'm sure they're just as customer-focused as they ever were. But their numbers are dwindling, if not disappearing altogether. Most of us, if we want fresh milk, have to go to the market ourselves and stand in line behind someone with a stack of coupons and forty-seven items in a ten-items-or-less lane, while their kids run up and down aisle six, and the scanner, of course, enters the wrong price again.

It's just not the same.

The Miraculous Powers of Pie

NO MATTER HOW FULL YOU ARE, you always have room for pie, right? But have you ever wondered, *why pie?* Why isn't there always room for beef? Or peas? What is it about pie that makes us willing to scoot everything else in our stomachs over to make room? What is it about pie that draws us under its power so easily?

Cake is different from pie. We can easily wave off a decadent five-layer torte, admitting that there is no way on earth we could eat even a single bite of it after a full meal. We take a Death by Chocolate cake to mean what it says, and so we retreat.

But pie is different. Pie appears lighter to us, as though we'll hardly notice it going down. We succumb to the temptation and go ahead and have a slice. Sometimes even two. We do this no matter how full we are. Again I ask, why?

I believe one thing that draws us to pie is its social significance. Some of the best conversations you'll ever have will be over a slice of pie. Cake doesn't lend itself to small talk as easily. This is due to the balance factor. Trying to maneuver a forkload of cake up to your mouth requires concentration—more concentration than is required of a forkload of pie. You can eat pie and converse with your dinner guests at the same time. With cake, you might be talking, but your focus will be on your dessert. You have to keep an eye on that wobbly bite of cake all the way to your mouth. People don't trust people who don't look them in the eye, so eating cake affects your conversation and, hence, your social life.

Pie is easier to maneuver to your mouth because it is stickier than cake, especially after you've eaten the frosting off the cake (which is the natural order of cake consumption). Dry cake is almost impossible to balance on a fork. It waits until you get it almost to your mouth, and then it jumps off. Pie, on the other hand, usually makes it all the way to your mouth without a single crumb falling onto your lap.

We also rationalize pie as the healthier choice when it comes to dessert. After all, fruit pie has all that, you know, *fruit* in it. Even though the fruit pie could also have twice the calories and four times the fat content, you tell yourself you're eating fruit (lemon meringue counts as fruit, too, right?), so it's okay. The pie crust might have a whole cup of pure lard in it, but the vitamin C in the three cups of strawberries cancels that out. Or so I've heard.

The only cake that even comes close to offering this level of healthy benefits is carrot cake; but then, you have the whole carrot thing working against you on that argument. Carrots have no business being in cake. Carrots are vegetables. How'd they make the crossover onto the dessert tray? Did some baker accidentally knock over a bowl of carrots into his cake batter one day and then try to cover up his blunder by adding nuts, raisins, pineapple and cream cheese frosting? Did he really think we wouldn't notice the *carrots?*

We noticed. That's because cake can't get away with the things that a pie can. We can put anything in a pie crust and call it pie. We can put a half-dozen eggs in pies to make custard or bacon and asparagus to make quiche—a cousin of the pie—and no one complains. But try slipping a few Brussels sprouts into your cake batter and you can kiss the State Fair blue ribbon good-bye.

I confess I love sugar-free pies. Especially now that there are so many more varieties to choose from. Sugar-free cream pies are my favorite. I could eat cream pies until the cows come home . . . or my veins lock up, whichever comes first.

When it comes to pie, everyone seems to have his or her favorite. My mother's favorite pie was chocolate with meringue topping. I have a son who is a pumpkin pie fanatic. He doesn't even wait for Thanksgiving to roll around; he loves it any time of the year. My brother's favorite pie is pecan. My husband's is raisin pie, made from the recipe of a dear friend of ours who passed away years ago. Thankfully, she let me print her recipe in a church cookbook, so the Clotine Waterson Raisin Pie lives on.

What is your favorite pie? If you suddenly found yourself in a pie-eating contest, what kind of pie would you like to see sitting there in front of you?

Pie is also responsible for bringing my husband and me together. One of our very first dates was to a restaurant that only served pies. When the waitress brought my slice, she accidentally tilted the dessert plate a little too far and the tower of lemon meringue pie landed squarely in my lap. A lot of dates would have been upset, but I felt sorry for the waitress. She must have been devastated. And besides, getting upset wouldn't make matters any better. I knew she would bring me a new slice, and I could also scoop up a good portion of the fallen pie, thus increasing my intake of lemon filling by at least ten finger-licks' worth. Make lemon pie out of lemons, that's what I always say.

Pie really does bring out the best in people. No wonder there's always room for it.

Up, Up and Away . . . But You're Going to Pay

THE AIRLINES ARE CONTINUING to find new ways to squeeze even more money out of us. Nothing demonstrates this more than a recent announcement by an Irish airline that it is considering charging a $1.40 restroom fee to all passengers. *They can't be serious.*

Unfortunately, they can be, and they are. I guess they're figuring that most airline restrooms don't have enough room for both you *and* your money, so you might as well drop it in the slot before entering.

If this new cost-cutting measure proves successful, other airlines could follow suit, or even implement other fees. It's not enough that they're now charging us for our luggage, our meals and even an extra seat if we can't fit between the armrests. They still want more. One day we might see the following fees become standard in the airline industry:

Air-Conditioning Vent fee: $10.00 (Any vent not paid for will be covered in duct tape.)

Oxygen Mask fee:	$25.00 ($50 if attached to oxygen.)
Seat Reclining fee:	$5.00 (Per one-eighth inch of movement; considering most airline seats only recline five-eighths of an inch, this should not be cost prohibitive.)
Call Button fee:	$45.00 (Fee doubles if button is pressed by accident.)
Beverage-Cart Injury fee:	$30.00 (We *told* you to keep your legs and elbows out of the aisle!)
Obnoxious Seat Partner Removal fee:	$60.00 ($150 if *you're* the obnoxious passenger.)
Overstuffing Overhead Compartment fee:	$40.00 ($3,000 if it causes aircraft to lean to one side and fly in a circle.)
Crying Baby fee:	$65.00 (Per five hundred miles of incessant screaming.)
Pillow and Blanket fee:	$35.00 (If either item tests positive for the Ebola virus, fee doubles.)
Peanuts and Pretzels fee:	$8.00 (Did you really think we'd be giving these away free forever?)
Safe Landing fee:	$100.00 (If landing is in the Hudson River, there will also be a $600 Captain Sully surcharge.)

These are just a few of the fees the airline industry could start charging us in the near future. And on our tightened budgets and limited retirement funds, this sort of thing can really pinch. If you've been putting off any travel plans, you might want to book your flight while you can still get seconds on those peanuts and pretzels . . . without too much begging, that is.

Weathermen and Cheese

I USED TO DO SOME comedy writing for Fritz Coleman, stand-up comedian and NBC's weatherman for the Los Angeles area. Fritz is a talented comic/writer/weatherman, and a very nice man.

I'll never forget one of my early encounters with Fritz. It happened during the taping of one of the Bob Hope shows. When the meal break came, I drove to a local fast food restaurant and ran into Fritz there. We shared some small talk about the day, the taping and whatever else came up. Then we said good-bye.

When I got in my car and looked in my rearview mirror to see if it was safe to start backing my car up, I couldn't help notice that a chunk of melted cheese from my burger had somehow adhered itself to my cheek. I was mortified.

I don't know if Fritz noticed it, but I don't see how he could have missed it. Most moles aren't orange. If he did notice it, though, he never said anything about it.

I bring up Fritz the weatherman because much of life is like the weather. Have you noticed that? You'll have periods of beautiful, clear skies and then, out of nowhere, a storm begins forming, and the next thing you know, you're dealing with a Category 5 hurricane.

When the storm passes over, the sun comes back out and the skies clear up. You assess and repair the damage, thank the good Lord you survived, and start all over again. We all go through this process at some time or another in our lives. If we live on this earth, we're going to have to deal with storms, both the weather kind and the life kind.

One day, though, if you're lucky, you'll look back on those areas that were damaged by the rain, winds and whatever else happened to come your way, and you'll realize they have all been replaced by something better and stronger. Chances are the next storm that comes your way won't be nearly as devastating because of what you learned from the ones that have passed.

Although the cheese-on-my-cheek incident certainly wasn't a storm, it has helped me weather similar situations that have since come my way. I now know to continually check my face for any spare food, both when I'm in the middle of eating with a business associate and when I'm simply driving down the highway hungry.

See, whether it's a major crisis or just another embarrassing moment in a lifetime of them, good usually does come out of bad.

I Miss Rabbit-Ears TV Reception

THEY WEREN'T BIG SCREENS or plasma or even Blu-Rays. But they had the capability of receiving a transmission and showing it on a whopping seventeen-inch television screen . . . well, at least most of the time, that is.

Rabbit-ear television sets were what many of us had back in the day. You remember them, don't you? Whenever the reception got a little fuzzy, all you had to do was walk over and tweak the antennas a little, and wa-lah—the picture would miraculously return, clear as a bell.

You can't do that with today's television sets. If the reception is fuzzy, you have to wait out the storm, call your cable company or your television repairman, or buy a brand-new set.

My father seemed to have the magic touch when it came to rabbit-ear reception. Not only that, he could use a wire hanger and get the same reception.

Wire-hanger antennas were a lot more common than you might think. Lots of homes had them, twisting and turning out of the television set like a couple of corkscrew willow stems.

Rabbit-ear antennas can hardly be found anymore, and I miss them—mainly, for what they represented. That spirit of improvisation. Of making do. Of perseverance. You'd move one rabbit ear to the right and then you'd move the other one to the left. If that didn't work, you tried bending or twisting them. And eventually, if you didn't give up, you'd have your picture. Ah, the good ol' days.

If you still have a television set with rabbit ears that you no longer want, don't give it a cold-hearted toss into the trash heap. Show some respect for the ol' guy. Lower its ears ever so gently, and give it a salute for all of us who remember its long and faithful tour of duty.

PROFILE: DAN KEEFE

Retired Los Angeles police lieutenant
Age: 61

Dan and his wife, Louise, braving the elements.

What is the most outrageous thing you've done since passing your fiftieth birthday?

Taking three months to pull a travel trailer clear around the United States and keeping to a schedule that allowed me to stay in bad weather pretty much all the way.

Is there anything you haven't done that you would still like to do?

I would like to win at least one argument with my wife.

What do you think is the single best thing about growing older?

Grandchildren.

Name one thing that you appreciate more with age.

Youth.

What would you say to those who have just reached or will soon reach retirement age?

Good luck, and once you've got your ducks lined up, watch out for the "goose."

Looking back on your life, what's the most important thing you have learned?

The most important thing I have learned is this: When all is said and done, when all the honors and successes of life have faded, when it gets to the point where memories take up most of your day—it was the people in my life that made it all worthwhile. Take more time to enjoy them while you can.

Part Four:
We're a Force to Be Reckoned With

Get Around, Get Around, I Get Around

COME ON, ADMIT IT. You've watched the commercials for those motorized scooter chairs, and although you might be completely mobile, you've been tempted to pick up the phone and order yourself one, right? Don't feel bad. I've found myself thinking the same thing. But then, if given the choice, who wouldn't take scooting along on a power chair over walking? Shopping malls, amusement parks, airports and even your local super-grocery store can all call upon your legs to do far more than they enlisted for. A motorized chair can save steps, energy and, most of all, the soles of your shoes. And bottoms of your feet.

Whenever I see a motorized scooter sitting there by the shopping carts at Walmart, it takes everything within me to pass it up and go with the perennial three-working-wheels-out-of-four shopping cart. But it's the right thing to do because I don't really need the scooter. At least not yet.

I'll also confess that I've been tempted to buy one of those at-home stair elevators. I usually think about it on my third trip up the stairs with an armful of clean laundry. The older we get, the steeper those stairs start looking, don't they? I have the same thirteen steps that I've climbed for years, but for some reason, they've started looking like thirty recently. A couple of times I think I saw snow at the top of them. That's why so many homebuilders are putting the master bedroom on the main level of the house now. They understand. As we get older, we don't care about going upstairs. Some people don't even know what they have on their second level until the movers come and haul it away to the next house. It's not uncommon to hear comments like these on a Boomer's moving day.

"So that's where we put the Christmas decorations."

"We have three more bedrooms up here? Why didn't somebody tell me?"

"Say, how long has that family been living up there?"

Front porch steps aren't any easier to climb. Frankly, I think there should be a limit of three steps for every front porch in America. In fact, it should be a law. Have you ever visited someone who had more front steps than the Taj Mahal—or at least it seemed like it? By the time you reach the top, you don't even have the energy left to ring the doorbell. You just lie there on the front porch huffing and puffing in a prone position, figuring they'll have to leave the house at some point and will find you. There's no telling how many Avon ladies have met their demise because of front porches like this.

A stair elevator would help with this problem. Maybe I can find a two-for-one special. One for inside the house, and one for outside.

As more and more of us are living longer and longer, who knows how many other helpful inventions are going to hit the market. It's comforting to know creative minds are thinking about us and how to make our lives easier. And just for the record, when it comes time for a motorized scooter, I'm putting streamers on mine.

AN OPEN LETTER TO DRIVERS WHO TAILGATE US

Dear Driver Who Won't Back Off Our Tail,

It has come to our attention—by looking in our rearview mirror—that we are apparently not driving fast enough for you. We apologize for this oversight on our part. We saw a sign a few miles back that stated the speed limit was forty-five mph. But because you are going around seventy mph and riding our bumper, we are obviously the ones in the wrong. We were not aware that seventy was the new forty-five.

We can tell by the look on your face that our driving at this speed is ticking you off. In fact, you might even think we are doing it intentionally. We can assure you that we are not. Sitting too long at an intersection after the light has turned green is what we do to intentionally tick you off, not driving too slowly.

We would pull over and let you pass, but as you can see, the road has no shoulder. You may feel free to go ahead and pass us if you like, but kindly refrain from honking your horn as you do so. There is no need to honk. We are not used to sudden loud noises coming from behind us. (We know what you're thinking, but that's not what we meant.)

If you will allow us our rightful space on the road, we will be forever grateful. However, should you refuse to alter your behavior, we will be forced to do the only thing we can do: brake for no reason at all. We don't want to meet you this way, but your actions will leave us no choice.

Thank you, and, oh yes, one more thing—the next time we see you on the road . . . eat our dust.

Sincerely,
The Driver of the Car in Front of You

The Perfect Match

HAVE YOU HEARD ABOUT THIS? Soon a matchmaking service may exist not for potential spouses but for potential airplane seatmates. That's right. No longer will you be forced to sit next to the seat partner of your nightmares. You can have the ideal seatmate by answering a simple questionnaire and letting a computer make the match for you.

I'm not sure what kinds of questions will be asked on the questionnaire, but I do know what important facts I would want entered into the database. My questionnaire would look something like this:

1. Have you suffered any recent relationship problem, and do you consider a two-hour flight free therapy?
2. When you're in a window seat, what is the greatest number of times you have gotten up out of your seat during a fifty-five-minute flight? (If your answer is in the double digits, you do not need to complete the questionnaire. Proceed directly to the rental car company of your choice. Some people weren't made to fly.)

3. Do you drool, snore or mumble while you sleep, and if so, would it bother you to be awakened by a whack on the head with an airline magazine?

4. Have you ever tried to sneak a snake onto a plane in your purse, and if so, would you be opposed to joining him in the luggage compartment of the aircraft?

5. Will you be traveling with a child under two with an ear infection and a piercing scream that dogs thirty thousand feet below can hear?

6. Do you plan on pointing all the air-conditioning vents in your direction, and if so, do you really think you could defend such a move against an overheated menopausal woman in an overcrowded airplane?

7. Do you plan on talking on your cell phone even after the flight attendant asks that all portable electronics be put away? If so, do you have a problem with said phone being tossed out of the aircraft?

8. Do you typically carry onboard your own meal of boiled eggs and Limburger cheese whenever you fly?

9. Do you understand the concept of bathing, and do you have any aversion, allergy or phobia that would prohibit the use of deodorant or mouthwash?

10. Have you recently taken a vow of silence, and if so, how long is the waiting list to be your seat partner?

I'm not sure if the airlines' questionnaire will be this thorough, but it's nice to think about, isn't it?

Makin' Do

MY FATHER WAS A CARPENTER, and his talents went well beyond those of any ordinary carpenter. He could make something out of practically nothing. He once made his own Christmas tree out of an old broom handle and branches that he had cut from the hedge in front of his house. The result was one of the prettiest "Christmas trees" I have ever seen.

Dad even made his own burglar alarm system once out of rope that he strung from the front inside doorknob up to the light fixture that hung over the stairs. The rope was then connected to a bucket of nails that he had strategically hung from the light fixture. His theory was that someone trying to enter the house during the middle of the night would pull on the rope, triggering the bucket to dump the nails to the ground, thus making a loud noise and waking everyone up. Granted, it wasn't exactly Brinks, but it would have done the job had anyone ever tried to break in.

My father even did a bit of his own at-home dentistry. Growing tired of his false teeth never fitting properly (they would fly across the room every time he sneezed), he decided he would try readjusting them himself. He'd hold the teeth over a burner on the kitchen stove and melt the palate just enough to get it pliable. Then he would reshape it until it was the perfect fit. Sometimes this would require melting and reshaping multiple times, but like any dedicated artist, he wouldn't stop until he was one hundred percent satisfied.

As I've already said, one of my dad's most impressive skills had to do with the ordinary clothes hanger. My father could twist and shape a clothes hanger until it would not only get him into a car that he had locked himself out of but would also get amazing reception for our television. It was the original HD (Hanger Definition).

He'd also use it to get reception on our car radio. My dad was the Michelangelo of the wire hanger.

My dad is no longer here, but every once in a while something reminds me of his stunning creativity: a notebook filled with pencil drawings of inventions he would have invented if only he'd had the time, construction plans for projects he wanted to do around the house, or a tool he had recycled by using the handle of one tool and the body of another.

Dad's can-do, will-do spirit still inspires me today. When times are tough, I can follow in his footsteps and incorporate this same sense of thriftiness into my own life. I may never do my own dentistry or hang a bucket of nails above my stairs, but I do have a talent for repairing broken things so they'll provide many more years of service.

Thanks, Dad, for the example of blending creativity and frugality. But then again, what else would I expect from someone who kept his sense of humor intact while living through the Great Depression?

I Miss the Old TV Shows

REMEMBER WATCHING television when comedies weren't mean, when they didn't make dads look like dufuses, and when they didn't have a political slant one way or the other? Remember when dramas were just great stories without any agendas? Remember when police shows didn't show so much violence but featured a guy in a suit asking for "Just the facts, ma'am"?

Remember the golden age of television?

Remember when Lucy and Desi didn't share the same bed on television, long before the days of almost-anything-goes soap operas and *Desperate Housewives*?

Those days will probably never return, but they hold good memories for us, don't they? Memories of a more innocent time, and a time when Ward and June Cleaver could solve just about any problem.

I miss those days. If you're a child of the fifties and sixties, I'm sure you miss them too.

When I was growing up, we didn't always have a working television set in our house, but I managed to watch a lot of the shows of that era. Whenever our TV was down, I'd find one to watch wherever I could, even if it was in the electronics section of a department store.

Television has played a major role in most of our lives. Some of my favorite shows were *The Honeymooners*, *The Munsters*, *The Addams Family*, *The Carol Burnett Show*, *The Andy Griffith Show* and *The Dick Van Dyke Show*. Have you noticed how a lot of the shows back then started with the word "The"? There were more, like *The Adventures of Ozzie and Harriet*, *The Adventures of Superman* and *The Many Loves of Dobie Gillis*. I also enjoyed *Hogan's Heroes*, *Gomer Pyle* and *The Red Skelton Show*. And I was a faithful watcher of animal-driven shows such as *Mr. Ed*, *Lassie* and *Rin Tin Tin*. I don't know if the "mice" in *Mighty Mouse* and *The Mickey Mouse Club* qualify as real animals, but then again, I don't think Mr. Ed could actually talk either.

I watched police shows like *Highway Patrol* and *Dragnet*, and espionage shows such as *Mission: Impossible*, *I Spy* and *Get Smart*.

We had westerns such as *Wanted: Dead or Alive*, *Gunsmoke*, *The Rifleman*, *The Lone Ranger*, *Raw Hide* and *Bonanza*.

There were suspense shows such as *The Twilight Zone* and *Alfred Hitchcock Presents*.

I watched just about every episode of *I Love Lucy*, as well as the Bob Hope specials and *Star Trek*.

I was a faithful fan of *Bewitched*, *Green Acres*, *The Beverly Hillbillies*, *Gilligan's Island* and *I Dream of Jeannie*.

Perry Mason was my grandmother's favorite show, and I'd often watch it with her.

We even had game and tribute shows such as *Queen for a Day*, *This is Your Life*, *To Tell the Truth* and *What's My Line?*

There were music-driven shows such as *The Monkees*, *American Bandstand* and *The Partridge Family*, and doctor shows such as *Ben Casey* (I had a crush on him) and *Dr. Kildare*.

There was no shortage of father-driven shows, either: shows such as *Make Room for Daddy*, *Father Knows Best* and *The Andy Griffith Show*. Of course, *Sky King*, *The Three Stooges* and *Little Rascals* were regulars in our house too.

And that's just the tip of the iceberg. There are plenty more that I haven't even mentioned yet—shows we all loved and enjoyed watching night after night after night.

When someone asks me what my favorite television shows are today, I can name only a few. But look at how many favorites we had back then. I'm not so sure any of those shows would make it today; they probably don't move fast enough for this generation of television viewers. But they were great shows to grow up with, weren't they? Thankfully, we can still catch them on some networks that specialize in nostalgia . . . or we can get them on DVD and enjoy them all over again. That's one good thing about progress. It moves life along, but it can help make the journey back a little easier too.

PROFILE: ALVIN FARLESS

General manager, operations for Sabreliner Corporation

Age: 69

"I am not wearing a helmet in this photo . . . that is my hair with fifty miles-per-hour hair spray."

What is the most outrageous thing you've done since passing your fiftieth birthday?

My wife JoAnne bought me a Harley Davidson motorcycle when I was sixty-seven. She did that because I told her if I did not get one soon, it would have to be delivered to my nursing home outfitted with training wheels. Recently I was riding it across Illinois on SR127 and was stopped by the Highway Patrol and told I was doing 101 mph. I told the officer the sign said 127 but I just couldn't get it to go that fast. I got a ticket.

Is there anything you haven't done that you would still like to do?

1) Grow older.
2) Ride my motorcycle to Sturgis.
3) Fly a plane through the St. Louis Arch.
4) Go on a six-month cruise.
5) Pay off Sears.

What do you think is the single best thing about growing older?

Every day you wake up with new friends.

Name one thing that you appreciate more with age.

I have two:

1) Restrooms.
2) Family. Be nice to them. You have to realize your kids will be picking your nursing home.

What would you say to those who have just reached or will soon reach retirement age?

Retire as soon as you can.

Looking back on your life, what's the most important thing you have learned?

Raise your kids in church. There is a lot of comfort at the end in knowing your family will meet you in heaven.

Part Five:

It's All in How You Look at It

The Upside of a Recession

HAVING MADE IT THIS FAR, chances are you've endured your share of recessions. Recessions come and they go. The problem is, when they go, they end up taking a lot of our money with them. But we can survive that too.

At the writing of this book, our country has been in a serious recession. Home prices have plummeted; CEOs of banks, car companies and insurance companies have been going to the government asking for a bailout. Even Donald Trump was having trouble getting a loan. Right now, times are tough.

By definition, a recession is a slowing down of the economy. It's a time when keeping up with the Joneses means beating them to bankruptcy court.

Money has been tight lately, but don't fret too much. As I'm sure you've learned by now, a recession doesn't have to be all bad. Believe it or not, some good things can take place in this kind of economic environment.

Here are just a few of the silver linings:

Hate crowded malls? In a recession, you get to have the whole place to yourself. And even land a premium parking space too.

Remember that overpriced house you wanted a few years ago? Now, you can get it for half the price. And they might even throw in their gas-guzzling SUV that's already parked on blocks in the front yard.

In a recession, you can have all the vacation time you want. (The downside is, it might come with a pink slip.)

In a recession, banks and financial institutions are finally forced to reduce the number of credit card applications they mail out. In other words, they'll send you only ten a week now, but three of those will be in your pet's name.

A recession gives you the opportunity to develop new skills, such as learning how to operate the change-counting machine at your local grocery store.

In a recession, you can't afford as much food as before, so you lose weight effortlessly. In no time at all, you'll be able to fit into that size eight dress that's been hanging in the back of your closet. Yes, the Financial Stress Diet has one of the highest success rates around. Whenever you feel like a snack, simply thumb through your stack of bills instead. It beats every appetite suppressant on the market.

Considering the typical savings account balance, if your identity gets stolen, who cares?

In a recession, people aren't as quick to give you their two-cents' worth. They simply can no longer afford it.

And lastly, in a recession, you get to meet a lot of former CEOs of major corporations that you otherwise wouldn't have met. They're now handing you your french fries and asking what kind of dipping sauce you want.

Advantages of Life over Fifty

DON'T THINK THAT simply because we've passed the fifty-year mark, life as we know it is over. Don't think that we can no longer "hang with our homies," because the truth is there are plenty of parts on us that are hanging lower than ever. Our skin for one. But even with all the bodily changes facing us, there remain plenty of advantages to passing our fiftieth birthday. Here are some:

1. Your senior discount is so close you can almost cry.
2. People keep bad news from you because they don't think your heart can take it.
3. You find out that *spending* your retirement fund is a lot more fun than *saving* it.
4. You can walk down the street talking to yourself, and everyone just thinks you're on a cell phone.
5. You get your money's worth out of the bulb in your left turn signal. (Who else has ever left it on for an entire road trip across America?)
6. Your limited view over the steering wheel provides greater protection for you from snipers.

7. When you cut the corner too tight with your motorized scooter and bump into that pyramid of canned goods at your local grocery store, the kid standing innocently nearby, watching the aluminum avalanche, will probably be blamed.

8. You sometimes get to go to the front of the lines at amusement parks.

9. You can have a hair-coloring disaster (blue, pink, purple, periwinkle) and no one will notice.

10. Liver spot outbreak . . . *can we say instant tan?*

AN OPEN LETTER TO THE AMERICAN TAXPAYER

Once the bailout money began to roll out, did you notice how a lot of banks, credit card issuers and other companies immediately had their hands out? Thankfully, lawmakers from both parties finally set some stricter guidelines on the money they were giving out. But maybe they should have asked them to do one more thing, such as write an open letter to the American Taxpayers, officially requesting the money. It would be sort of a Letter of Hardship and loan application rolled into one.

It might read something like this:

Dear American Taxpayers:

We, the undersigned bankers, car manufacturers, mortgage brokers, money managers, credit card companies and other interested parties, do respectfully request a loan/gift/ransom paid by you, the American Taxpayer, over your lifetime and the lifetime of generations to come, to help us out in this time of economic uncertainty.

We realize that we are asking for billions of dollars, and that is a lot of money. We further realize that you are no doubt recalling that time when you asked us for $53.75 for your tab at Applebee's, but your credit card was declined because it would have pushed you over your limit by nineteen cents. Because you had already eaten the food and were treating a business client, our actions caused you embarrassment. We sincerely regret that. We should have at least allowed your client's meal to go through. But that was a long time ago, and we hope you have moved beyond the petty bitterness of the past and will not hold that little incident against us.

We hope, too, that you will not decline any of our future spa retreat expenses in like manner. If you can find it in your heart to overlook some of our colleagues' bad sense of timing in regard to their previous spa trip . . . okay, two spa trips . . . okay, three spa trips (apparently, some of them are slow learners), we would all greatly appreciate it. In fact, most of us feel so bad about what AIG did, that the rest of us are going on a spa retreat ourselves to discuss the matter further.

We would also like to mention that if, after the initial loan of however many billions of dollars we happen to need, we find ourselves in a position of needing additional funds, please allow us that flexibility. If you will recall, there was one time when we did let you go $1.50 over your credit limit so that your house payment would go through. True, we charged you a $39.00 over-the-limit fee, but we went ahead and gave you the buck and a half, didn't we? Now, we are asking for similar consideration. $1.50 . . . $700 billion, it's all just money, right? Are you really going to quibble over a bunch of zeroes?

And speaking on behalf of the Big Three automakers, they would appreciate another loan from you as well, to help bail them out. They also hope you will overlook their behavior that one summer when you were out of work, and you had those medical bills piling up, and they called you at all hours of the day and night with threats of repossession, taking your firstborn as collateral on interest, and possibly your right kidney. In their words, they were "just kidding."

We also noted that you are requiring personal financial information from us so that you can determine whether we can afford to pay back the note. That's so cute. We only make someone jump through those kinds of hoops when they want to borrow money from us, not the other way around. Silly you. In our defense, though, every time we have asked you for three references of someone who has known you since birth, your tax returns since high school, every bank statement you've ever received in your life, and the amount of allowance your parents gave you in the fifth grade, that was for your own good.

We trust this letter has convinced you of our need for the multibillion-dollar bailout from your taxpayer money. If you will do this for us and help us get back on sound financial footing, we promise that things will be different in the future. For one thing, once we get the money, we have already determined that we won't be lending any of it out to anyone. This, we feel, will prevent us from making the same mistakes again.

We wish you the best in the coming year. Thank you for listening to us. Kindly refrain from using your credit cards, and don't be late on your car payment, or we will have to revert to our old ways. Also, on your most recent credit card statements, please note that your limit has been lowered and your interest rate increased as our gift to you. No need to thank us. It's the least we could do.

Sincerely,
Your Friendly Credit Card Company

I Miss the TV Test Pattern

IT'S HARD TO BELIEVE, but I think I miss the test pattern. Remember when the networks went to bed for the night and left the test pattern on the television screen (the original screen saver), letting you know that programming was finished for the night so you could go on to bed and get some sleep? There weren't any twenty-four-hour news programs or shopping networks that let you spend your money at three o'clock in the morning, if you so chose. People went to bed.

Nowadays, something is always airing on television. On hundreds of channels. All over the world. It hardly seems right to call the late night talk shows "late night" anymore. Late night is well past eleven-thirty, according to a lot of people's schedules and insomnia.

Not me. After eight o'clock, I'm scoping out my pillow. It doesn't matter if my favorite movie is being aired, or if some political crisis is happening at home or abroad; I'm going to bed.

I'm sure the all-night programming helps a lot of people: shut-ins, people with sleeping disorders, college students looking for a distraction from their homework. I'm just saying, I think I prefer the days of the test pattern. It was good for us. It limited our television consumption. Television was a terrific invention, but with all the channels and programming available to us today, do we really need *this much* of a good thing? And what about all the entertainment that isn't all that entertaining? There are a lot of shows that many of us could have done without very nicely.

When only the test pattern was on, you read yourself to sleep. When only the test pattern was on, you talked to your family. When only the test pattern was on, you finished your homework. When only the test pattern was on, you didn't buy things in the middle of the night (unless you sleepwalked and happened to find a store open). The test pattern gave you time to unwind, think and maybe even say your bedtime prayers.

The test pattern was like a "lights out" call at camp. It meant the day was over and it was time to turn in. Tomorrow would be a brand-new day. There was a clear division between today and tomorrow. Monday didn't blend together with Tuesday, and Tuesday with Wednesday, so the entire week felt like one giant day. Tomorrow and today were separate days, and we knew it. We closed down one and prepared to open the next one.

I miss the TV test pattern.

Wisdom Comes with Age

A LOT OF WISDOM comes with age. The CEOs of all those failed mortgage and investment firms should have asked the Middle-Class Boomer for advice before doing some of the things they did with the money, such as accepting outrageous bonuses or going on spa retreats while their companies were in the midst of collapsing. Because of this poor sense of timing and judgment, I thought it would be a good idea to pass along a little wisdom that comes only from those with a lot less money and a few more candles on their birthday cake.

Middle-Class Boomer Advice for Ousted CEOs

1. If you feel you must celebrate the government bailout, don't go to a spa and spend $440,000 to do it. Celebrate where the middle class celebrates—Denny's. It doesn't go over all that well with the American public if, while we're losing money in our retirement accounts and home values every day, you're out getting a massage on our dime, or a pedicure, and making us foot the bill (pun intended).

2. Don't give yourself a hundred-million-dollar bonus for driving your company out of business. If you truly feel you deserve

a bonus for something like that, give yourself the kind of bonus our bosses give us—a fifty-dollar gift certificate to Walmart.

3. You don't need a mansion in the Hamptons, one in Palm Beach and another one in Beverly Hills. If you're having such a hard time deciding where to live, do what the middle class does and buy yourself a used RV.

4. Sell your yacht and buy a bass boat instead. If times get real bad, you'll be able to catch your own dinner like many of us do.

5. Speaking of food, give up the expensive caviar. Chocolate tapioca looks the same and tastes better. And it's a lot cheaper.

6. Sell your Lear jet and fly commercial. I'm sure plenty of Americans would love to sit next to you and have your undivided attention on your next four-hour flight.

7. Trade in your limo on the government's Cash for Bentleys campaign and, as financial guru Dave Ramsey would say, buy yourself a "beater." It won't take as much gas, and it'll be a lot easier to maneuver as you go around the drive-through lane at McDonald's.

8. You don't need to golf all the major courses in the world. Do what the middle class does—go to your local Putt-Putt and hit that ball to your heart's content. Anyone can avoid a sand or water trap, but try hitting the ball over an erupting volcano or down the drawbridge of a castle. That takes real skill . . . and a lot less money.

9. Fire your butler. You don't need him. Follow the lead of the middle class and live by the motto "If you make the mess, clean it up."

10. And finally, don't be embarrassed when you're standing in the unemployment line. The middle class won't look down their noses at you. In fact, I'm sure a lot of people at the unemployment office right now are gladly saving you a spot.

Geezer Alert

I COULDN'T BELIEVE MY EYES. I read the article over and over. But no matter how many times I read it, none of the letters in it were changing. The story was right there in front of me and the news wasn't pretty. According to said article, the "young and hip" were leaving the social networking site Facebook because it was now filled with "old geezers over thirty."

Say what? Old geezers *over thirty?* Are they *serious?* When did thirty-one become the new eighty-one?

This is nothing against Facebook, social networking, or even the young and hip—or to put it another way, the-young-and-clueless-as-to-how-quickly-they-are-going-to-be-over-thirty-themselves. My issue is simply with the words "old geezers" and "over thirty" and the fact that they've been put together in this way.

Thirty isn't anywhere near old geezerhood. These days *seventy* is nowhere near geezerhood.

What does "geezer" *mean* to a twenty-year-old anyway?

Do they think geezers sit around all day and watch the weather channel? We, the Baby Boomer generation, don't even do that. Not all day, anyway. Only when there's a storm . . . somewhere on the planet. And we never sit through the same forecast for more than four or five repetitions.

Okay, next?

That geezers wear their pants too high on their waists?

Sure, they can laugh at us now. But the next thing we know they'll be wearing them that way themselves and calling it cool. They already stole our baggy pants look. Can't they come up with their own styles?

Next?

That geezers go to all-you-can-eat buffets?

We have two words for them: the economy. Okay, two more. *Free seconds.*

Next?

That geezers are always adjusting their hearing aids.

Like they're not always adjusting their iPod headphones?

Next?

That geezers get cranky when things don't go their way.

Like they get when their cell phone drops a call, or when we're not moving fast enough in front of them, or when Starbucks gets their coffee order wrong?

Sometimes you have to help people see the light, to show them the truth about some of the incorrect statements they make.

Geezers aren't thirty-one, thirty-two, or even forty. In fact, "geezer" isn't an age at all. It's an attitude. Sure, you can have it in your middle and senior years.

But you can also have it at twenty. The "right" social networking site doesn't make you hip. Some of the coolest people I know are seniors.

Most twenty-year-olds couldn't even keep up with them.

You Say Good-Bye, I Say Hello

LAST YEAR A LIFELONG FRIEND of mine received what you would think on the surface would be devastating news. She was told she had an inoperable malignant brain tumor, and that without treatment she would have only a few weeks to live. With treatment, she might have at best ten months.

After much thought and prayer, and family discussion with her husband and daughter, she decided to take the treatment.

As sad as this news was to everyone who knew her, my friend Martha had one of the most amazing attitudes I have ever witnessed in the face of such grim news.

"When God says it's time to go," she told me over the Nashville-to-Los Angeles telephone call, "I'm going to put my hand in the Lord's and step into eternity with Him. I'm ready to go whenever He says. I'm open to His will, whatever it is."

Wow. With all of us around her trying our best to hang on to whatever hope we could, praying that the diagnosis would change by some miracle, she was as calm as if they had just told her she needed some dental work.

Where does that kind of peace come from?

Martha knew beyond any doubt in her mind that she would soon be going to a better place.

In the midst of all the uncertainty in the world today, this woman had certainty. She was open to staying around here on earth, of course, should the treatment work. But she was also resolved to accept that she had come to the end of her life.

She told me on the phone that night that she was happy with the life she had lived. Her only daughter had recently married, and even though Martha would have loved to be here to one day welcome a few grandchildren into the world, if that wasn't God's path for her, she would accept it.

Martha and I went all the way back to my junior high and high school days. She was such a dear friend that she was considered part of our family. She even spoke at my mother's funeral, and that night on the telephone, she reiterated her feelings about her relationship with my mom.

"I will never forget your mom. My family didn't go to church, so when I started attending on my own as a teenager, your mom made it a point to make me feel welcome. She would come looking for me wherever I was sitting, and she made sure that I knew I was fully accepted. She was my first friend at church. You'll never know what that meant to me. I probably wouldn't be walking with the Lord today if it wasn't for your mother."

This was over forty years later, and my friend still remembered the kindness of one lady. Not only did it make me proud of my mother, but it was a reminder of the power that each one of us possesses—the power to change someone's life with one simple act of kindness.

We may not be able to give a lot of gifts away, especially right now due to the uncertain economy, but the gift of kindness doesn't cost a dime. And after hearing a tribute like that forty years later, you can't argue with the shelf life of kindness.

Martha lived about a month after her original diagnosis. She left this earth far too quickly. But that was on our timetable. She was ready to go—excited, really.

I hope she said hi to my mom for me.

PROFILE: DELORES MORGAN

School bus driver and motorcycle safety instructor for the state of Pennsylvania

Age: 71

What is the most outrageous thing you've done since passing your fiftieth birthday?

My dear husband, Leonard, let me travel by my Honda Gold-wing motorcycle in all fifty USA states . . . although, in Hawaii and Alaska, I rented a Harley. Eighty percent of the time I traveled alone, with God changing my guardian angels every two hours. I slept in barns, cemeteries, under picnic tables and in the homes of many friendly people. I stayed in very few motels (they're not free).

Is there anything you haven't done that you would still like to do?

I sponsor several girls through World Vision in India and would like to go there for a visit someday. Maybe go on an elephant safari.

What do you think is the single best thing about growing older?

Looking back and seeing what God has done in my life in protecting and guiding me. Our difficulties in life are not always as bad as we think, and we can learn from each one.

Name one thing that you appreciate more with age.

My health.

What would you say to those who have just reached or will soon reach retirement age?

Plan what you can do for others. Keep a quiet time for yourself. Also, try new things: take up art, cooking, sewing, woodworking, church choir; help clean the church; do whatever, but do it all with gusto! Give a few smiles away each day. Talk to teens and encourage them. These days, they need it. We all do.

Looking back on your life, what's the most important thing you have learned?

To forgive the ones who have hurt me. This, then, lets me move on with my life. Don't worry about the things you cannot control. And learn something new every day.

Part Six:

A Few Minor Adjustments

Playground for Boomers

DOES ANYONE KNOW why there aren't any playgrounds for adults anywhere? I'm not talking about Branson or golf courses or anything like that. I'm talking about *real* playgrounds, with swings and slides and such. Do the powers that be think we wouldn't use them? If they do, they are so very wrong.

How many times have you sat on a playground bench watching your grandchildren play, only to look up at the chain holding the swing and ponder whether it could hold your weight? Let's be honest—the thought has crossed your mind a time or two, hasn't it?

All they'd have to do is post a sign that said "For use by children of all ages, one to one hundred," and we'd be out there playing every day, whether the grandchildren were with us or not. We'd be swinging on the swings, riding the teeter-totter, and climbing on the jungle gym for hours—or at least until the toddlers got their mommies to make us stop and let them have a turn.

I don't know about you, but my inner child is alive and well and just waiting for permission to take a spin on a tire swing or go down a slide head first. (Okay, maybe not head first. Now that I think about it, that sounds like it would hurt. But going down the regular way sounds fun.)

Some parks do provide separate workout areas for adults and teenagers, but they are usually only a set of parallel bars and some gymnastic rings to swing on. We want fun things to play on. Basically, what we want is a McDonald's PlayPlace for Boomers.

When did we start believing that grown-ups didn't need this kind of fun anymore? Community park planners need to take a visit to Disneyland and watch adults on the merry-go-round, Alice in Wonderland ride, or even Space Mountain to understand that adults *love* reliving their childhood.

What would happen if someone put in a swing set at a retirement center? I have a feeling many of the residents would love it. Up and back and up and back. I can see it now. I can even see some seventy-year-olds twisting in the swing until it winds all the way up to the top, and then letting it unravel, spinning them like a top, until the ride finally comes to a stop.

Provide something like that, and who knows what impact it would have on their disposition. One thing's for sure—they'd probably go to bed that night with a smile on their faces, eagerly awaiting the next morning when they can do it all again.

My Over-Fifty To-Do List

NOW THAT I AM over the fifty-year mark, here is my new to-do list. From this day forth, I shall . . .

1. Pretend to be hard of hearing so I can find out what the people around me are really thinking.

2. Order the smaller portions from the senior menu . . . and then, ask for seconds.

3. Attend weddings of people I don't know, simply for the refreshments. What will I do if someone asks how I know the bride or groom? See #1.

4. Not waste time with negative, critical people. The average person listens to tens of thousands of words a day. Life just goes better if most of those words are positive.

5. Watch the news; then watch *Dr. Phil* to find out how to cope with what I've just watched on the news.

6. Learn something new, such as how to speak a new language. Or just settle for becoming fluent in Text Messaging Shorthand.

7. Ride buses and subways just to see who'll stand up and give an exhausted older woman his or her seat. Then, when we stop, get off and jog to wherever I'm going.

8. Remind myself to feed the cat.

9. Remind myself I don't have a cat.

10. Watch *The Doctors* to see what new symptoms I need to look out for. You have to be careful with this, though. I once thought I had a flesh-eating bacteria attacking me. It turned out to be an herbal facial mask that I had forgotten to remove.

I Miss Dressing Up

REMEMBER WHEN we used to dress up for social events? There was no such thing as "business casual." We dressed up for work, church, the theater, dining out and even travel. Have you noticed that hardly any of us do that anymore? We barely dress up for weddings and funerals.

What happened?

We relaxed. But maybe a little too much.

Like most everyone else, I love the comfort of casual wear, yet I am convinced that we lost something when we started stuffing our dresses, suits and formal wear into that never-never land of plastic garment bags and forgetting all about them.

Even Easter isn't what it used to be. You hardly see hats anymore. I like hats. They're fun. It's hard to feel down when you're wearing a great big floppy spring hat. Maybe that's one reason there's so much depression in the world today. We're not wearing enough hats.

Men don't wear ties as much as they used to, either. I can't blame them there, though. Ties are surely uncomfortable. Who started this whole tie thing anyway? What fashion designer said,

"Hey, guys, let's all wear a noose around our neck, and let's make it match our shirts." That made sense to someone?

Bow ties are dressy. That's why you often see them paired with tuxedos. But only a dwindling number of men wear bow ties on a regular basis these days—a few news reporters, accountants and maybe some chemists. A bow tie is a lot like the spring hat. It's hard to feel sad when you're wearing either one.

Dressing up makes people feel special. It can change someone's outlook when they're down. It can alter how they carry themselves. It can make them act and feel classier, more sophisticated and more confident. It can turn an ordinary night into an extraordinary night. If dressing up can do all of this, why, then, aren't we doing more of it?

That's one of the nice things about cruises. Most cruises offer at least one formal night. Passengers get to dress up in evening wear and enjoy a fabulous meal, great service, and a journey back in time when formals and tuxedos at dinner were not all that unusual.

Remember how you used to love to dress up when you were a kid? At least we girls did. It was fun to go through our mother's, or our grandmother's, closets or trunks, and put on the fanciest outfit we could find. Then, we'd wrap as many necklaces around our necks as we could without falling over and pretend to be high society.

Dressing up was fun. It still is. Find an occasion to do it again.

Bearing Gifts

I'VE ALWAYS LOVED giving gifts to people. Receiving them is fun, too, but not nearly as much fun as giving them. I usually start my shopping for the following Christmas on the twenty-sixth of December.

I've given gifts to people who never acknowledge them. Why? Because even if they don't acknowledge them, it makes me feel good. I've been doing this as far back as I can remember.

This gift-giving compulsion no doubt relates to my childhood. To this day I can remember the feeling I used to get when I would rush into the living room and find a pile of gifts that my parents (make that "Santa") had secretively loaded in there sometime during the night. The sight of those gifts was both amazing and mysterious. Amazing because there were so many, but then again, there were seven of us in the family. Even two gifts each would have created a mountain. And it was mysterious because we lived in a small house, so where had my mother and father been hiding all those presents during the year? I suspected the garage, but we often played in there and I never saw them.

Christmas shopping is easier when you're shopping for kids. Kids tell you exactly what they want. And their gifts usually come in large boxes, so the gift size always looks exciting. Shopping for adults, or teenagers, is a bit more challenging. I like to get people what they want, so I try to listen throughout the year to hear what they might tell Santa if they weren't too embarrassed to sit on his lap.

Even President Obama had a bit of trouble in the gift-giving department. Remember when he went to England and presented the Queen with an iPod? I gave an iPod to my granddaughter a few Christmases ago, but I never thought of sending one to Her Majesty. I didn't even realize she was in the market for one. Who would've known?

Actually, the President's present might have been the perfect gift for the Queen. I understand it was filled with photos and memories of her previous trips to the United States (I guess this was in case her disposable camera wasn't working at the time). But even if the camera had been working, the Queen probably wouldn't have been in any of her own photos, anyway. You know how moms and grandmas are always left out of the shots because we're the ones holding the camera and snapping the pictures? So in that way, President Obama's gift might have been a good choice.

The President even had some cool songs downloaded onto the iPod for the Queen. I'm not sure if "We Are Family" and "God Save the Queen" were among them, but she might have liked them.

Also, if you'll remember, during that visit a bit of controversy arose over the fact that First Lady Michelle Obama put her arm around the Queen. Apparently, this otherwise friendly gesture broke from royal protocol. You are not supposed to do this sort of thing to the Queen of England. But from the news clips I saw, it appeared that the Queen put her arm around Michelle, too, so it may have been all right. Who knows? It could have been that in the challenging economy facing the world that day, the Queen needed a hug. And anyway, it's not as though they high-fived each other.

Still, some members of the press, and especially the foreign press, had a field day with this. They thought it was improper to break with traditional protocol. They also thought the iPod was in poor taste. But Monday morning quarterbacking is easy. Finding the right gift to present to foreign leaders has to be challenging. What do you get someone who has everything, including their own country? It's hard enough to find the right gifts for our teenage grandchildren, much less for kings and queens and other foreign dignitaries.

If there isn't one already, I think a Gift Czar to handle these kinds of things for the White House would be helpful. This would keep the current President, and all future Presidents, from making any more gift-giving faux pas.

And speaking of gift faux pas, we can't deny that giving back the bust of Winston Churchill that England had presented to us wasn't a good idea. First of all, the usual thirty-day return window had passed, so right there President Obama should have known this wasn't a good move. And then, there's the whole regifting issue. If you are going to regift a gift, you never want to regift it to the person who gifted it to you in the first place. This breaks all basic regifting rules and leaves you wide open to embarrassment. A Gift Czar would have foreseen this crisis in time and intervened.

I don't know who would be a good pick for Gift Czar, but probably not a member of Congress. Even though many members of Congress have proven they know how to give gifts without strings attached, they have a tendency to go overboard and give out too many of these gifts. I'm sure we can find someone for this task, but we'll need to do it quickly, or the Queen could be in line for a GPS and the first season of *Desperate Housewives* this Christmas.

So the next time you're trying to figure out what to get your pre-teen granddaughter, your college-bound grandson, or anyone else on your gift list, remember, you're treading in dangerous waters. There's a reason Santa only does it once a year. So choose wisely. And if you need any help, feel free to call. I'm an expert at this sort of thing.

And just for the record, I would have kept the Churchill statue.

When One Door Closes, It's Usually on My Foot

MOST OF US ARE FAMILIAR with the saying, "When one door closes, another one opens." Some of us may even live our lives by it. But if we're honest with ourselves, we could probably look back over the years and recount as many instances when one door closed and the next one slammed shut on us too. Some weeks we may have even had to deal with a whole hallway of doors with "Closed" signs.

That's life. We're not always greeted with "Welcome, come on in."

It's been my experience, though, that most doors slam for a reason. Those shut doors keep us from going in a direction we weren't meant to go in, or keep us moving on down the hall until we get to the door that's intended for us.

My life almost went in an entirely different direction, but thankfully, I didn't give up. I continued to walk on by one closed door after another until I found an open one. Sometimes, I didn't even know what I was looking for; I just saw the open door and walked through it.

For me, that open door was writing. I never dreamed I would become a writer, at least not as an occupation. I enjoyed writing and, according to my schoolteachers, had a talent for it. But writing as a profession wasn't in my plans.

Looking back, however, I can see it was in Somebody Else's plans. I wrote my first "book" when I was nine years old. It was about being the youngest child in a family of five kids, and it was titled "No Fun Being Young." It was a humorous take on my life up to that point, and I still have that dated and slightly worn-out composition book.

I also collected "Mommy, Mommy" jokes. Remember them? They were all the rage back then.

"Mommy, Mommy! Why is Daddy running so fast?"

"Shut up and reload."

They weren't the most sensitive jokes, but as kids we would repeat them to each other and giggle ourselves silly.

Between the years of twelve and fourteen I was into both reading and writing poetry. I had a book of poetry that I read just about every night (I'm fairly certain I have the cover of that book somewhere). The poems I wrote during that time were taped to the wall above my bed. I taped some twenty to thirty poems up there. Had there been a coffeehouse in our neighborhood, I might have been down there reading my collection, safely disguised behind a pair of sunglasses and a beret. But there weren't any coffeehouses; just a coin laundry, a pharmacy and a Piggly Wiggly grocery store (and I couldn't get other shoppers to stand still long enough to listen).

Even with my strong desire to write, I pursued a secretarial major in high school. I enjoyed typing, shorthand and bookkeeping, and . . . well, you know how it goes. You're getting good grades in certain classes, so the school counselor thinks that's the natural direction for your life. I was destined to be a secretary. Never mind that I also enjoyed my English and Creative Writing classes, a secretarial major was the path for me.

After high school, I worked as a clerk typist at an insurance company, and then later took a job as a church secretary. The church secretary job was one of those doors that lead to other doors. One door led to the next and to the next and to the next, until I was right where I was supposed to be.

As a church secretary, I was given the opportunity to try my hand at writing. In fact, my pastor suggested I write a Christmas play one year. I did, and enjoyed it so much that I continued writing plays, comedy songs, and, on occasion, even a "roast" of our pastor or anyone else who was celebrating a special event in their life. Like the famous Friar's Club or Dean Martin roasts, these banquets became one of the highlights of our church, with deacons, the choir director, the church treasurer and anyone else who wanted to get in on the act joining us on the dais. Often, I'd do a slide show down memory lane, filled with outrageous photos and funny captions. The pastors enjoyed these roasts more than anyone, and I enjoyed the laughter of the audiences. Little did I know that this was the door I was always meant to walk through. It led me to writing professionally, and I even used my secretarial skills of typing, filing and general office work in the process. Funny how doing what you were created to do often incorporates much of what you've been learning, without your even knowing why you were learning it.

If you're still looking for what you're supposed to be doing in this stage of your life, and if doors have been closing on you, one after another, after another, don't give up. You weren't supposed to walk through those doors. At least not yet. Your door for this time in your life might just be down the hall a bit. So keep on walking and trying those doorknobs. One of them will open eventually, and it'll be the right one.

I Miss Stars without Attitudes

REMEMBER WHEN ACTORS and musicians had to spend years working their way up the celebrity ladder, fine-tuning both their craft and their attitude through years of hard knocks and stage experience?

Today, it seems all they need is a good scandal. Or a YouTube video. Stars are born seemingly overnight. Resumes are often padded, and some have no problem conjuring up personal histories for maximum sympathy. Example: "My mother was a half hour late once for picking me up after ballet class" becomes "I was abandoned by my parents." Or "I spent the night at a roadside rest stop because I was too tired to make it to the next city" becomes "I was broke and had to live in my car."

Most stars of yesterday didn't have such entitlement issues, nor did they seek sympathy. They knew where they came from, they honed their craft, and they had greater appreciation for whatever good fortune came their way. They also had a keen awareness that it could all be gone tomorrow. They took seriously that old theory of "be nice to the people on your way up the ladder because you're going to meet them again on the way down."

Back then you didn't become a celebrity simply because you got into a fight with the paparazzi, had a drug overdose or carried your dog around in your purse. Reality didn't make you a star; talent and hard work did.

I miss those days. Although I imagine the dog's enjoying the attention and the fun of riding around in a purse. As for all the little doggie outfits? Well, maybe it's time for an intervention.

PROFILE: PEARL SUTPHEN

Had two careers, working at Elmira Knitting Mills and
Benedict's

Age: 98

Pearl with turkey that she shot

*What is the most outrageous thing you've done since passing your
fiftieth birthday?*

On May 30, 2008, at the age of ninety-six, I shot a turkey (see
photo above).

At the age of ninety-seven, I played Minnie Pearl in a Jug
Band.

Is there anything you haven't done that you would still like to do?

I seem to be content at my age.

What do you think is the single best thing about growing older?

You can make more decisions about what you do, and rest more.

Name one thing that you appreciate more with age.

Good health.

What would you say to those who have just reached or will soon reach retirement age?

Watch your health, and stay active.

Looking back on your life, what's the most important thing you have learned?

To love life and people and keep busy. Also, to be friendly, love the Lord, go to church and read my Bible.

Part Seven:

Traditions, Habits and Memories

I Miss Landlines

I MISS THE GOOD OL' DAYS when everyone had a landline. You didn't have to cut a call short because you suddenly "lost connection." You never had to worry about your call catching someone at an inopportune moment. Such as the joke that circulates around the Internet about a woman (or sometimes it's a man) who goes into a public restroom and suddenly the person in the stall next to them starts asking them questions. Not wanting to be rude, they answer each one, until finally, the caller says, "Hey, I can't talk to you right now. The idiot in the next stall keeps answering me."

That story has been recounted by numerous comedians claiming it happened to them. Only the location changes. It has been set at an airport, a roadside rest stop, a department store, a school and who knows how many other places (good stories travel fast). But the tale is funny and it does prove a point: life has certainly changed since the advent of the cell phone.

There has been speculation of late that the telephone landline may soon go the way of VHS tapes. More and more people are dropping their landlines altogether and depending on cell phones for all their telephonic needs. I understand this, but saying goodbye to this old friend is still kind of sad, isn't it?

I remember growing up with a big, black clunky phone with a rotary dial. Dialing the phone number took forever, especially if it included a lot of nines or zeroes. That phone was so big we even had a special chair with a side table attached to it just to hold the phone.

There were no area codes back then, either. We had seven digits, and that was it. To this day, I remember my phone number from my childhood. Funny, I forget my age at times, but I can recall that phone number.

When they added the area codes, many of us wondered how we were going to memorize all those numbers. Now look at us. We're keeping all sorts of phone numbers, passwords and access codes in our memory banks.

If we go back even further in time, we'll arrive at the days of the "party line." I can remember my grandmother having a party line. On a party line, one or more families shared a single phone line. You'd have to listen for your special ring to know whether the call was for you. Because party lines were on the honor system, the other person on the same line in a completely different house across town could easily pick up their phone and listen in on your conversation. Back then, the telephone company trusted us to mind our own business.

I'm sure most people did.

Okay, they probably didn't. But then again, there weren't as many channels on TV back then. What else were they supposed to do for entertainment?

When Princess phones first came out, they were all the rage. These were slimmer versions of the big, black clunky phone, and they came in a variety of colors. You were considered cool if you could upgrade to a Princess phone. We kept our black clunky phone for years, so that should tell you what my "cool" quotient was back then.

Wall-mounted telephones were another new development. This made a telephone table unnecessary, but it also presented a health risk. Sure, the extra long cords that often came with them could stretch from room to room, but if you wandered too much while talking on the phone, you could soon find yourself tied up in a Ma Bell cocoon.

To avoid this dilemma, the phone company followed with the cordless phone. This was wonderful because it permitted you to talk unrestrained, as long as you didn't wander too far away from the phone base. But those first cordless phones were so big and clunky, carrying them around with you was like carrying an anvil with a dial tone.

Fast forward several decades and along came the smaller, more convenient cell phone, and they've been shrinking ever since. Today, cell phones can be smaller than a credit card; and some even work like pocket computers, giving you access to the Internet and your e-mail accounts.

Cell phones have also brought back the personal ring tone, only this time without the party lines. With speaker phones and the propensity for people to carry on their entire cell phone conversations within earshot of anyone who cares to listen, who needs party lines?

With the ever-advancing world of technology, who knows what kinds of phones will be available to us in the future? The way technology is advancing, there's no telling.

And just think—it all started with Alexander Graham Bell making that first call to Dr. Watson back in 1876, saying, "Watson, come here, I want you." As they say, the rest is history.

So, yes, I do miss everyone's having a landline. But progress is progress.

Who are we to stand in its way? But for the record, I'll take that old rotary phone over a sleek cell phone any day. With the landline you had to stay in one place when you talked, so the person on the other end of the line received your full attention. You could also balance the receiver on your shoulder when your arm grew tired of holding it. And last, but not least, there was the dialing. On some days, that dialing was my only form of exercise.

Twelve-Step Program for Buffet Addicts

THE TWELVE-STEP PROGRAM has helped hundreds of thousands of people overcome different addictions. With no irreverence intended toward this fine program, I believe the Boomer generation could benefit from another Twelve-Step Program tailored specifically to them. A Twelve-Step Program for Buffet Addicts. Health officials are just beginning to recognize the severity of this addiction and its effect on the otherwise unsuspecting middle-aged and senior population. Because of the urgent need to address this problem, I am providing the following steps to buffet addiction recovery:

1. Admit that you are powerless over fried chicken legs and gizzard gravy.
2. Believe that a power greater than you is pulling you to the yams and cinnamon butter.
3. Make a conscious decision to turn that third plate back over to the waitress. Just because you *can* have all you can eat, doesn't mean you *should*.

4. Take an inventory of yourself and your handbag. Any muffin you find that you did not enter the restaurant with should be returned.

5. Admit to God, yourself and another human being the exact number of calories you consumed in your last buffet experience, and how close that figure is to the national deficit.

6. Be ready to be intercepted by the manager on your way to the ice cream machine. It's for your own good.

7. Know your "ladle limits." The idea is not to drown your salad with the blue cheese but to simply dribble the dressing over it. If you cannot resist the temptation to overindulge, you will need to have the temptation physically removed from you.

8. Make a list of any and all persons that you may have cut off in line or unintentionally offended by snatching the last chicken wing out of their hands before they could maneuver it onto their plate. Be willing to make amends.

9. If possible, go ahead and make amends to each one of these people, unless they are bigger than you and still noticeably upset over your insensitive actions.

10. Continue to take a regular assessment of your buffet desires and whatever success you've had in resisting them.

11. Share this new knowledge with other buffet addicts, so that they, too, can kick the all-you-can-eat habit.

12. If you find you truly can't stop going to buffets, then go on and go. All I can say is I tried. Oh, and save me a seat!

A Little Bit Country

WHY IS COUNTRY MUSIC SO SAD? I love it, but it can be depressing, can't it? I don't know if it's the songs or the passion with which the singer belts out the tune that makes the words so heartbreaking, but listening to a country song without a lot of tissues on hand is nearly impossible. I think that could be why Kleenex has their manufacturing plant in South Carolina, just a state away from Nashville. They understand.

It's been said that country music is "three chords and the truth." I agree. Country music writers "get it" that life is too short to beat around the bush. Say what you want to say, and then move on, as Reba McEntire did in "For My Broken Heart" or Hank Williams did in "Your Cheatin' Heart." If you were close to making it when she walked out, just say it like Rascal Flatts did in "What Hurts the Most."

Even if your dog dies in your arms, you can sing about that, too, the way Elvis did in "Old Shep."

The most heartbreaking song of all time is about someone who never did get over their lost love. George Jones's "He Stopped Loving Her Today" is a whole river of tears just waiting to happen.

Three chords and the truth—no wonder country music continues to thrive today. The supply of song ideas is endless, because the supply of truth and pain and disappointment in life is endless.

But the supply of other truths is endless too. There's the truth of living each moment of your life to its fullest, as in Tim McGraw's "Live Like You Were Dying." There's a son's memory of his dad, as in Alan Jackson's "When Daddy Let Me Drive." There's a dad's heart for his daughter, as in "Stealing Cinderella." There are tributes to love that last through the ages, like Josh Turner's "Would You Go with Me?"

And there is even a tongue-in-cheek tribute to country music by Rascal Flatts, called "Backwards," which says that if you play a country song backward, you get your house, your truck, your dog, your best friend, your wife, your hair, your pride and your life back.

No wonder country music is just as popular today as it was in our day. It knew how to put the truth to music, three chords at a time.

I Miss Christmas Carolers

I LOVE CHRISTMAS CAROLS. In fact, I believe we've lost something by the lack of carolers strolling down our streets during the holiday season. You used to be able to count on at least one group of festively dressed singers showing up on your front porch step. But it's been years since I've seen carolers on mine, or on any street for that matter.

I guess we all just grew too busy. Or not enough of us were handing out the "figgy pudding" after a few choruses of "We Wish You a Merry Christmas." Or it's been too cold. Or too rainy. Or too . . . well, go ahead and fill in the excuse du jour.

I miss the carolers, though. And I'd like to start a campaign here and now to bring them back to our streets. Of course, I might have to update a few of the carols to accommodate the times, especially in light of the recent downturn in the economy. So, here are some suggestions:

(Rewrite of "O Christmas Tree")

O Christmas tree.
O Christmas tree.

I wish I could afford you.

* * *

(Rewrite of "Jingle Bells," beginning with the verse "Dashing through the snow.")

Flying to DC
In a private, corporate jet,
Asking for a loan
To help us pay our debt.
If you'll bail us out,
We'll cut expenses now.
Those nice folks from AIG
Are going to show us how.

* * *

(And the chorus to "Jingle Bells.")

The Big Three
The Big Three
Chrysler, Ford, GM.
We're the next in line for help,
'Cause our future's looking grim.

We admit,
Flying here
Was a stupid stunt.
But this time we *drove* our jets.
They're double-parked out front.

* * *

(Rewrite of "I'll Be Home for Christmas.")

We'll be broke for Christmas,
Most of us agree.
Our stocks have tanked,
Our hopes all sank
For presents 'neath the tree.
Christmas Eve will find us
In one collective pout.
We'll be broke for Christmas,
'Cause no one bailed *us* out.

* * *

See, traditional Christmas carols can still be a lot of fun. We just have to hit the streets and start singing them. So grab your winter coat, your earmuffs and scarf, and start caroling again. I'll put some hot chocolate on for you.

A Good Tradition

IN THIS AGE of electronic communication, I still enjoy sending and receiving Christmas cards. I hope the tradition never stops. Even if you don't hear from someone all throughout the year, getting caught up with his or her life during the holidays is a pleasant feeling, isn't it?

I especially enjoy photo cards. You get to see how families have grown and how everyone is looking these days. Growing older with good friends is a nice feeling.

One thing that never ceases to amaze me is how seldom I receive duplicate cards. Have you noticed this phenomenon? There can only be so many Christmas cards on the market in any given year, and yet, how many of us receive duplicates? Have you thought about the odds of this? I open card after card after card, from people all over the country and even a few from foreign countries, but rarely do I find a duplicate. (I'm also amazed at how seldom a duplicate dish turns up at a church potluck. Obviously, it doesn't take much to amaze me.)

Back to Christmas cards—another reason I love them is that they conjure up all sorts of good memories for me. I remember reading my mother and father's Christmas cards and then pinning them up on the living room draperies (the cards, not my mom and dad). That was where my mom always displayed her Christmas cards.

Christmas cards were like the social newsletter. You could read about all the goings-on of family and friends during the previous year.

Some people even include a holiday letter with their card. Holiday letters give you the year's news, but in greater detail:

Dear friends and loved ones,

It's been an eventful year. Our fourteen-year-old daughter Miranda finally got her braces this summer. It put us back a bit, but because she's only got the two teeth, we all figured they'd look better together. And no surprise here—Grandma Florence got more plastic surgery done. This time, it was a full body pull. Yep, they just scooted her skin on up her body a bit and then snipped it at the top. Remember that mole she used to have on her neck that looked like a relief map of Italy? It's now on her forehead. But the good news is she can hide it under her bangs (see enclosed family photo greeting card).

And speaking of the family photo, we apologize for the gaping hole in the top row, third person from the left. That used to be Uncle Chester's wife Agnes. If you haven't heard, none of us are talking to her anymore. Not since she ran off with the vet who was treating her bovine.

In closing, like so many others across America, George was laid off this month. So now Cousin Billy, who hasn't worked in twelve years, is making more than all of us with his aluminum-can recycling hobby.

And how was your year?

> *Happy holidays!*
> *The Persnickle Family*

The best thing about Christmas cards is how much encouragement they can bring. If you're looking for a way to make a difference in someone's life, put that person on your Christmas card list. Think of a person at your job, church or school, in the military, or even in your own extended family who might not receive many, if any, Christmas cards, and then send them one. You have no idea how much that little act of kindness could mean to someone. Finding an unexpected Christmas card in your mailbox, with a warm and friendly greeting, can make your day. It's especially meaningful if it's the only card you receive. Too many singles, seniors, soldiers and others don't hear from anyone during the holidays. And when you think about it, changing that only costs the price of the postage. Where else could you spend so little and make such a difference in someone's life?

So open your Christmas cards this year, look at them often, and enjoy every sentiment. Appreciate the fact that someone took time to send you a holiday greeting. Send your own cards to your family and friends, and try to remember to send one to someone who least expects it, to remind them they're thought about too. You'll feel good about it, and I can guarantee you it'll make someone's day.

A Cake of Fruit

WHILE WE'RE ON THE SUBJECT of the holidays, have you ever found yourself wide awake in bed in the middle of the night wondering how the tradition of fruitcake started? Me neither. But I have wondered about it whenever I've walked by a fruitcake display at my local grocery store or watched a couple of men in brown try to dolly a tin of it up to my front porch.

So I did a little research.

Apparently, the origin of fruitcake dates back to the ancient Romans. (Gladiators probably threw it at each other in the arenas. They knew if they survived that, the lions would be a piece of cake . . . pun intended.)

To make fruitcake, the Ancient Romans would stir pine nuts, raisins and pomegranate seeds into a thick batter. Then they would cook it. The resulting fruitcake might be one of the reasons for the demise of the Roman Empire.

I understand that they're testing some of the ancient Roman ruins to see if any of the stones and bricks could have, in fact, been fruitcake. Given its shelf life (Expiration date: Eternity), this would have been a good choice for building material. The dessert is virtually indestructible.

During the Victorian era, the cake was regularly served at tea parties. This could also explain why, during this time, ladies wore those big hoop skirts and puffy sleeves. It gave them a place to hide the unwanted slices.

Today, fruitcake remains a popular holiday gift (for the giver, at least), and an even more popular regifting item. Some fruitcakes have been passed around among families and friends for years, even decades.

You may not be aware of this, but December 27th has been named National Fruitcake Day. (Over the years, some people have confused National Fruitcake Day with some political election days, but they are clearly different.)

I'm not sure why the fruitcake needs its own day, but apparently it does.

I also understand that January 3rd is Fruitcake Toss Day, which sounds a little dangerous to me, especially because the cake has recently been classified as a possible weapon of mass destruction.

So, if you happen to get stuck with one or more unwanted fruitcakes this next holiday season (or already have been), here are a few ideas on how to get rid of them.

Ideas for Discarding Unwanted Fruitcakes

- Rebuild our nation's bridges with them.
- Fill all the potholes on Interstate 40 with them.
- Use them to build schools, hospitals and churches capable of withstanding tornado and hurricane-force winds.
- Send them to NASA. If they can make a fruitcake weightless, our lead in the space race will be guaranteed.
- Use them to train our Olympic weight lifters. We'll win the gold every time.

- Donate the recipe to Goodyear for their research in making longer-lasting tires.
- And finally, if you can't find anything else to do with them, send them to Sarah Palin for skeet shooting.

All I have to say is, if Osama bin Laden is hiding out in a bunker made of old fruitcakes, we'll never find him.

Living in the Now

IF YOU DON'T LIVE IN THE NOW, you're either stuck in the Was or you're fretting over the What Ifs of the future. You should be living in the Now. Living in the Was makes you look back, and looking back not only causes you to miss out on much of your Now, it also gives you a crick in your neck.

On the other end of the spectrum, living in the What Ifs will wear you out worrying over what could happen but probably won't.

Think about it—after a tragedy, most people say they never saw it coming. The things they were worrying about weren't the things that ended up happening. In other words, what did, in fact, take place wasn't even on their radar.

If we've learned anything by this point in our lives, it is this: we can't predict how life is going to unfold. We simply have to take it one joy, one crisis, one moment at a time.

We can't change our Was either. All we can do is learn from it. Spending so much of our Now regretting our Was is futile. It is energy wasted. Of course, we could have done some things better, avoided some disappointments had we only (you fill in the blank). And some people we sought love from never gave it. Looking back we see it all—the good, the bad and the "What in the world was I thinking?" We're going to regret some financial decisions we made and be relieved about some we didn't make. We're going to wish some people had never crossed our paths and thank God for the days other people did.

I like to look at life like this: Was is like the trash bin on our computers. We can file every bad thing that ever happened to us in there and in one motion dump it all, choosing to go on with life and never think about those things again. Or we can go back in and selectively take out the memories and lessons we want to keep and then move on from the rest. We're in charge of what we do with each and every file of our lives.

Instead of simply deleting those files that caused us pain, we might need to take another look at their contents. We might find some beautiful memories in there along with the bad ones. As the old saying goes, we don't want to toss the baby out with the bathwater. Some of those painful things in our past have been good for us. They've taught us lessons we'll never forget, and they've forced us to grow, even if only in the "I'll never let someone treat me that way again" department.

By the time we've reached middle age, one hopes our eyes will have been opened to one important truth in life. Forget what we may have thought as teenagers—we now know we're not the only ones who have to deal with life's problems. Everyone has had their share. We've all had to face certain challenges and deal with regrets. We have all had more disappointments and pain than we ever signed up for. Yet we've also been blessed way more than we deserve.

When troubles come, if we resist the temptation to isolate ourselves from one another, thinking no one could possibly know how we feel, and if instead we reach out to someone else, an old friend or a new one in the making, we might be surprised to discover how much we have in common with our fellow travelers.

We're all in this life together. Since the beginning of time, I don't think anyone went through their allotted time on earth without feeling some of the pain associated with the human experience. Just about everybody you meet can give you the name of someone who has let them down, someone who has backstabbed or lied about them, someone who has cost them dearly, and a friend who wasn't there for them when they needed it most.

Hate your job? You'll have company there too. You'd be surprised at how many people don't feel fulfilled in their career choice. That's why the second half of life is so much more fun than the first half. You finally can start to pursue your own dreams if you haven't already.

But you won't know how many others are just like you until you start sharing your frustrations, your disappointments, your hurts and your hopes.

We all have circumstances we wish had turned out differently. We have choices we made that we wish we could get a do-over on, and problems we didn't see coming.

But isn't it nice to know we have so much in common with each other? Through both the good times and the bad times, we're not alone in our journey.

PROFILE: GARY "THE LOVED ONE" HARDING

Retired Los Angeles County sheriff

Age: 67, but still on the right side of dirt!

What is the most outrageous thing you've done since passing your fiftieth birthday?

I took a river-rafting ride with my grandkids down the Truckee River. The ride was so hair-raising for me that my hair actually turned gray halfway through the ride. It was ugly; I was left with a sunburn, muscle aches, and cuts and bruises in places that I cannot even remember. At the end of the ride, although I was in so much pain I wanted to rewrite my will right then and there, my grandkids all jumped out of the raft and said— you guessed it—"Opa, let's do that again!" Of course, my wife

Sunny thought the whole thing was very funny and was busy snapping pictures of the entire disaster.

Is there anything you haven't done that you would still like to do?

I love to fly and would love to fly an ultralite plane someday.

What do you think is the single best thing about growing older?

Not having someone telling me what to do, where to go, and what to wear. After retirement, my definition of formal wear is a T-shirt, shorts and sandals.

Name one thing that you appreciate more with age.

Are you kidding? *Living!*

What would you say to those who have just reached or will soon reach retirement age?

Probably the same that I would say to most folks: Stay active and do *not* start just sitting in a rocking chair . . . it's a sure way to die.

Looking back on your life, what's the most important thing you have learned?

This may surprise you, but like most grandparents I now know for certain that I am smarter than Mr. Einstein. I do not disrespect his knowledge, but come on, as a grandparent today we have to know all about computers, computer games, text messaging, ever-changing electronic equipment and even the changing phone system. Ol' Einstein never had to deal with any of this. Who knew? Who knew all this would one day be required of us . . . right when we're supposed to be slowing down. Yes, we older folks have to be smarter than Einstein!

Part Eight:
We Sure Didn't See This Coming

Going Tubing

I ONCE SAW A CARTOON that pictured a pharmacist handing a man a giant tube of medication. The tube was so big, it could barely fit on the counter. To the best of my memory, the caption went something like this:

"Rub this on everything within one hundred yards of your house."

I know the feeling. Since passing the fifty-year mark, the number of tubes in my house has been multiplying at breakneck speed. I'm not sure what it was about my fiftieth birthday that started this whole ordeal, but it is real and can no longer be denied.

Our bathroom looks like a Smithsonian exhibit of the evolution of the tube. We have tubes of every shape, size, content and age. There's a tube for my husband's eczema, another tube filled with a salve for minor burns, and a tube marked Preparation something or other. We have hair products in tubes, toothpaste and teeth whitener in tubes, several tubes of hand cream, a topical antibiotic in a tube, and, of course, all the tubes whose labels have long since worn off—I have no idea what's inside of those.

I have so many tubes, when the grandkids rush in to announce they want to go "tubing," I immediately wonder if they've been into the medicine cabinet. I breathe a sigh of relief when I realize they're only talking about the water park. (Although a few of the tubes in my medicine cabinet are big enough to float on—down a lazy river.)

This tube collecting is new to me. Other than sun lotion, lip cream, and Bengay on occasion, I don't recall using this many tubes when I was younger. Same with my husband. He says all he had was a lone tube of Brylcreem in his high school years. Now look at us.

Travel gets a bit tricky when you're taking along an armful of tubes. Don't even think of putting them in your carry-on luggage. You'll never get them by Security. They'll make you toss them out so you can't commit mass-moisturizing of the crew and passengers, a crime punishable by up to five years in prison or a work-release program with a skin-care counselor. It's just not worth the risk.

Oh well. I guess tubing goes along with the aging process, so we'll just have to get used to having a lot of tubes around the house. It's probably only going to get worse with each passing year. So the best thing we can do is go with the flow . . . er, I mean . . . squeeze.

If a Woman's Hair Is Her Glory, Why Am I Tweezing My Chin?

I HAVE A WILD HAIR that keeps showing up on my lower-right cheek every couple of months. I'm not sure why it does this. As far as I know, I haven't encouraged it in any way. In fact, I usually trim it back as soon as it gets long enough to position between the blades of my scissors for a quick snipping. You'd think that would discourage it from its growth spurts. But so far it has been determined to stake its claim on my cheek.

Admittedly, there have been times when I've forgotten it was even there only to later discover the hair had gone to seed and was now doing mazelike growth patterns down to my chin.

Why, in the name of all things depilatory, does this sort of thing happen to those of us over fifty?

Good question.

I recall my mother battling the Attack of the Chin Hairs. so maybe it's hereditary. It was sad to watch her fight this problem, because no matter how many times she annihilated the enemy, reinforcements kept showing up. Just when she thought she had gained ground, a seemingly endless supply of even tougher troops were waiting just over the horizon (or just under the epidermis).

No matter how dedicated one is to the elimination of this enemy combatant, chin hairs are not easily deterred.

Again, the question is *Why?*

If you don't want to go with the hereditary theory, we could look into a hormonal possibility. If we're growing hair on our bodies where hair heretofore hasn't grown, maybe we are hormonally imbalanced. Maybe the delicate balance between estrogen, testosterone and progesterone is sorely out of whack.

Whatever the reason, I don't appreciate being able to do rope tricks with my chin hairs. I don't even watch that many westerns.

I suppose I should be thankful that I didn't have a chin-hair problem in my teen years. Who wants a prom picture like that? I'm also glad it wasn't an issue in the child-rearing years, either. Toddlers have a habit of grabbing onto any hair that happens to be dangling down in front of them, and a fistful of chin hairs in the hands of a two-year-old has "Ouch!" written all over it.

For most of us, chin hairs seem satisfied to make their first appearance after our fiftieth birthday. Maybe they think by then our eyesight is starting to fade and we won't notice them. Or maybe they think we've mellowed enough by that age that we won't freak out at the sight of them. Or maybe they have a sick sense of humor and think it's funny to jump on the menopausal bandwagon along with certain other body parts.

If you're battling your own chin hairs, several options are available to you. You can ignore them and allow them to grow wherever and however long they please.

Or you can remove them.

Removal techniques are varied. For years, tweezers were the weapon of choice. The downside to this is you can also get a piece of skin in the plucking process. This is not fun.

Shaving is another option. Depending on the density of the hair, you can choose from single-blade, double-blade, and ride-on shavers.

Hair removal cream works, but many of the products smell like rotten eggs. Unless that's your perfume of choice, you might want to stay away from those.

Waxing is one more form of unwanted-hair removal. But a lot of screaming tends to be involved in that process. If you live in an otherwise quiet neighborhood, I wouldn't recommend it unless you can handle a SWAT team encounter.

Electrolysis is yet one more process that's available. Electrolysis is supposed to be more permanent, as is laser hair removal. They say either of these procedures could take several treatments, but once you've removed all of the hair follicle, you should never be bothered with that unwanted hair again.

. . . Until it starts showing up in your nose and ears.

I Miss Drive-in Theaters

REMEMBER THE OLD drive-in movie theaters? They're practically nonexistent these days, but once upon a time they were all the rage.

I suppose we should have seen the end of the drive-in theater coming when they started holding weekend swap meets there. The drive-in was never intended to host a swap meet. It was a theater. An entertainment center. It wasn't much more than a parking lot with hundreds of speakers connected to metal bars, but it had a mysterious and compelling quality. It was like Stonehenge, only with popcorn.

The drive-in didn't need sixteen screens like theaters have today. A few drive-ins tried that multiscreen concept, but it was too distracting to be watching a Disney film with your kids on one screen while some slasher movie was playing on the screen to your right. So that concept died a quick death.

Other things made the drive-in experience different from the walk-in theater. For one thing, you could adjust the volume yourself. You didn't have to look over anyone's head to see the screen, either. And if you wanted to, you could even get out and sit on the roof of your car. If you were lucky enough to have a truck, you usually backed into the parking space and sat in the bed of the truck to watch the movie.

And when's the last time you bought a whole pizza at the movies? You could do that at the drive-in. The trick was to make it back to your car while balancing the box of pizza, five cups of soda, three hot dogs and an order of nachos. Then you had to remember where you were parked.

The downside to the drive-in, I suppose, was the propensity to drive off with the speaker still connected to your car. That sort of thing happened more often than most of us will admit. I'll own up to doing that once or twice. It gave a new meaning to taking the message of the movie home with you.

Lost

HISTORY DOESN'T SUGGEST that I have the best sense of direction. When I was young, I walked home from school by myself one day and got completely lost. I turned right when I should have turned left. It was only a two-block walk, but I ended up a lot farther away from my house than that. It's amazing how far you can travel in the wrong direction when you're looking for home.

Modern technology has given us devices we can put in our cars to keep us from getting lost. All we have to do is enter the address of where we're going, and the device directs us there. It shows us where we need to go, and most of them even talk to us. The best part is, if we make a wrong turn, it doesn't nag us until we reverse our direction the way a backseat driver might do. The mechanical voice gently informs us that we have simply made an error and asks us to turn around whenever it is safe.

Once, while attending a conference in Anaheim, California, I scoffed (to myself, anyway) at the rental car clerk who was trying to talk me into renting a GPS along with the car.

"No thanks," I said. "I grew up here. I know my way around."

After I realized Anaheim wasn't where I had left it, I called the hotel's 800 number to ask for directions. They told me that from where I was, I still had a long way to go. "Just keep going," the man said.

I'm a trusting soul, so I did what he told me to do. I continued to drive. And drive. And drive. When I hit San Juan Capistrano and started seeing signs for San Diego and then Mexico, I knew I had definitely gone too far.

I pulled over and called the number again to make sure he was leading me to the right hotel. This time, the clerk (a different one) told me that I had gone past it, and I needed to turn around and head back in the other direction.

He seemed to be directing me to a different hotel, maybe even a different universe, so I questioned him.

"I'm not going to the one that's by Disneyland." I said. "You're not sending me there, are you?"

"Lady," he said. "I'm going to get you to the right hotel. Trust me."

So again I trusted. I followed the directions and, to my surprise, they did lead me right to the hotel, just like he said. And it was the wrong hotel, like I had said.

Too tired to leave now, I just stayed, figuring I would drive over to the right hotel first thing in the morning. Which I did. At last, I had found the right hotel. Unfortunately, the room they gave me had someone else in it.

Back to the hotel clerk for another room.

The conference was fun, but afterward, when driving to visit my sister who lives north of Los Angeles, I got lost again. I drove all night all over Los Angeles, going miles out of my way and then turning around and driving miles out of my way again. I did this at least four times, because the exchanges for several major freeways were closed and I had to take alternate routes. If you're familiar with the Los Angeles area at all, they were the exchanges to the

5 and the 405. These are major freeways. You don't shut down their exchanges, both on the same night. Who would do such a thing?

I finally found a freeway that would take me north, so I got on it. That's all I knew how to do. Everything was starting to look familiar again, and I felt at ease.

That is, until I saw the flashing lights behind me. Now if you're a woman all alone in the middle of the night and getting pulled over, your first thought is, *Is this really a cop or some psycho impersonating one?*

It turned out to be a real cop. I explained that I had been driving around lost for hours. "I'm just tired," I told him. "Very, very tired."

He was gracious and told me to stop in at Denny's and get some coffee to help keep me awake. I told him I would, thanked him, and continued on toward Denny's and my final destination. I had left the convention before eleven o'clock. It should have taken me around two hours. It was now 5:30 in the morning.

GPS? Naw, I used to live in Los Angeles. I know my way around.

Aches and Pains

UNTIL I PASSED THE AGE OF FIFTY, I had no idea how many different places I had on my body that could hurt. I'm not talking about serious pain. I'm talking about your average, run-of-the-mill, everyday, drive-you-up-the-wall kind of discomfort.

I can certainly understand stubbing my toe and getting a shooting pain afterward. Or walking into a coffee table with my shin and feeling the immediate discomfort of that.

But to be sitting there watching television, minding my own business, and be hit with a shooting pain that comes for no reason and sends your popcorn raining all over everyone within a twelve-yard radius, what's up with that? The pains don't seem serious, just annoying. And startling. Couldn't we get some kind of a warning for these things?

Pain is something that, up until the middle ages (ours, not society's) has usually come from an injury or some other inciting incident. We get toothaches because we have a cavity. A migraine might follow a weekend of chaperoning a youth camp, but again, that's understandable. A number of ailments can cause a pain in our side, including appendicitis or gallstones.

But when your eye suddenly starts twitching all on its own, your leg cramps up in the middle of the night with no warning whatsoever, or your elbow feels as though you just hit your funny bone (only you didn't, and there's nothing very funny about it), the blame for these unfortunate incidents often belongs to the . . . ahem . . . aging process.

For the record, there really is no way to describe the pain of a muscle cramp. Only those who have experienced one can fully grasp that unique feeling that your muscle is trying to rip itself out of your body the hard way. I never realized toes could spread out that far away from each other and form such interesting pretzel-like shapes.

I don't know if any pain is equal to that of a leg cramp. Childbirth comes close, but I don't recall hitting the same high note then that I've been known to hit in the middle of a muscle cramp.

Obviously, you should check with your doctor to determine the cause of such pains, but if it proves to be the A-word (aging), I guess we just have to grin and bear it. And keep the aspirin close by.

No Accident

IF WE'VE MADE IT this far in life, chances are we've had our share of automobile accidents. My first one came when I was barely three months old. I wasn't driving.

My father was. It was Christmastime and my family was heading home after visiting my uncle and aunt. While stopped at a stop sign, we were hit head-on by a drunk driver. Our car rolled into the ditch and the accident nearly took my father's life. He was trapped in the car and had severe injuries. My mother was injured too, as were most of the family. I had a broken arm, but no one knew that until later when our relatives who were taking care of me noticed that I cried whenever anyone moved my arm.

I'm happy to say that all of the injuries eventually healed.

I was in another car wreck a few years back in the city of Houston. We had just finished putting on a comedy event, and three carloads of us headed to a restaurant for a bite to eat.

Again, while we were parked at a red light (maybe that's not such a safe place to be), we were hit by a car speeding down the road. The car hit us with such force, we rear-ended the car in front of us, and then they rear-ended the car in front of them. Then to add insult to injury, the driver took off. We could hear her mangled and broken car parts crunching together as she went on her way into the dark, rainy night. She didn't even stay long enough to see if we were all right. No one in our car was even moving, but she didn't care. Although I was wearing a seat belt, the impact sent me to the floor with the seat belt now wrapped around my neck. One of my shoes had flown off and was somehow wedged between the dashboard and the windshield on the driver's side. The driver, comedian Donna East, was lying on the collapsed seat, unable to move. Comedian Bob Nelson was in the back seat, covered in glass.

One of our friends chased after the escaping car by foot, trying to get a license number. Thankfully, another car joined in the pursuit and did manage to get the numbers. Someone called an ambulance, too, and it wasn't long before we could hear its siren in the distance.

I've been in a few more accidents, but by far, those two were the worst.

Now I've just added another one.

It happened one night on my way home from the pharmacy. I was driving, and my husband decided at the last minute to go with me—a decision I hope he doesn't regret.

As we rounded a curve on a back road near our house, I hit a patch of black ice, did a complete 360-degree turn, and slid off the pavement and into a telephone pole. I couldn't have scored a more accurate bull's-eye had I been aiming for it. But I wasn't aiming for it; it just happened. In one amazingly surreal instant, time stood still. We were powerless.

I looked over at my husband, who had his head down, both praying and watching the road disappear beneath us. Then I saw the telephone pole behind him, as we slid closer and closer to it. I thought of breaking out into a chorus of "Jesus, Take the Wheel," but it all happened too fast. I don't know how the driver in Carrie

Underwood's song managed to work in a whole verse and a chorus before impact, but for me, there just wasn't time. Before I knew it, we were one with the telephone pole.

Being from California, I am not used to ice, at least not as a driving surface. But ever since moving to the South, I had heard about the treachery of black ice on the roads in cold, wet weather. I never wanted to experience that feeling of having no control over which way my car was going. But now I have. And all I can say is that gliding on ice in an automobile is not nearly as much fun as doing it in ice skates.

Thankfully, our injuries appeared to be minimal. The car took a good hit, though. The front-right side was mangled, and the windshield had been reduced to a sheet of crushed glass. When my husband and I replay the accident in our minds, we have to thank God that it wasn't any worse. We are especially thankful that no traffic was coming from the opposite direction. And that telephone pole, as unyielding as it was, might have saved us from flipping over after sliding down the embankment.

Several people stopped and offered to help us, but my husband told them that we'd probably call a tow truck. Unfortunately, when we did, the towing company told us we would have a forty-five minute wait. With the temperature dipping further and the cold air freely coming in through the new hole in our right passenger window, we wondered if we had done the right thing by waving off our helpers.

"If it'll start up, I might be able to back the car out of the ditch," my husband said. "Then maybe we could drive it home."

That sounded like a good plan. But just as he was starting to figure out how to do that, a man and his young son drove up in their full-sized truck and offered to pull us out. Perfect timing.

"You'll never be able to back it out of there," he said. Then he invited me to sit in his warm truck with his young son while he and my husband figured out a Plan B.

The man moved some big rocks that were at the front of our car, and my husband was then able to drive the car forward and out of the ditch. I rode in the truck while the man followed my husband to make sure we all made it home safely.

"That's a nice car," he said, looking at the undamaged rear view of our vehicle.

"Thanks. And it was almost paid for." I laughed.

"It's just things," he said. "Just material things. It can all be replaced."

"You've got that right," I agreed.

"What's important is right here. . . . " he said, motioning to his son, who sat next to him all dressed up in his karate uniform. "Your kids. Family. That's what's important."

It was easy to see how proud this dad was of his son. Then, he continued. "We lost his mother two weeks ago. Material things don't mean a thing."

Already shaken up from the accident, I had to choke back the tears. His words amazed me. Here they both were, in the middle of their own fresh pain, reaching out to help a total stranger. It was cold outside, and rainy, and it was about dinner time too. They had plenty of reasons to give themselves for not stopping. But they stopped, anyway.

Throughout our lives, each of us has no doubt had the misfortune of meeting our share of rude, unloving, self-focused or self-righteous people. Meeting the other kind is so refreshing. I certainly met several of the other kind that night, especially that man and his son. That boy's mother would have been proud of them both.

PROFILE: MARY KOLADA SCOTT

Artist and newspaper editorial operations manager

Age: 58

What is the most outrageous thing you've done since passing your fiftieth birthday?

Taking up painting in my fifties and having my first solo art show at age fifty-seven. I had always wanted to be an artist but had been sidetracked by writing and raising a family. When I experienced the empty nest, I decided to pursue something I wanted.

Is there anything you haven't done that you would still like to do?

Travel abroad and visit my ancestral roots in Ireland and Slovakia. Publish a book of poetry. Build a larger studio.

What do you think is the single best thing about growing older?

Being forced to look inward because outer appearances are altered. My eyesight is on the blink but not my insight. Stop looking in the mirror and focus on something that matters.

Name one thing that you appreciate more with age.

My sense of humor. The doctors can cut everything else out, but as long as I retain that, I'll be okay.

What would you say to those who have just reached or will soon reach retirement age?

Try something new: another career, sport or hobby. It will renew your passion, stimulate your brain and give you a reason to keep moving forward.

Looking back on your life, what's the most important thing you have learned?

To focus on myself and to make my dreams and goals a priority. I didn't learn this soon enough and am making up for lost time.

Part Nine:

Reflections This Side of Fifty

I Miss Unorganized Sports

IF YOU'VE EVER SAT through an organized sports game with your own children or your grandchildren, especially one where some parent ended up getting into a shouting match with the coach or umpire, or worse, you've no doubt felt the same thing I have on occasion: Whatever happened to the simplicity of *un*organized sports?

Remember the good old days when all it took to have a baseball game were a group of your friends, a ball and bat, a few mitts, and something to pass as bases?

Remember when you could skateboard all over town, and the thought of jumping over a trash can or sliding down a stair rail on your board never occurred to you?

Remember when you could get up a basketball game in an instant with whoever was hanging out at the park, and football didn't require a test for steroids plus a signed release from your parents, your doctor, your career counselor and your attorney?

Remember summers when you would run down to the local swimming hole or pay thirty-five cents for a two-hour session at the local park pool? Now kids have their own memberships at gyms and health clubs and are in training for the Olympics as soon as they start walking.

I'm not against organized sports; I think they're great. All I'm saying is whatever happened to just playing a little baseball and no one keeping score? Or shooting some hoops, without the dream of March Madness even entering a player's mind? Why can't kids be kids? They don't always have to be in training for something, do they?

When I was young, we had a tetherball in our backyard. I love tetherball, but it can be a rough game. You could get hit so hard in the face by the ball that your cheek would sting for a week. It sure taught you the importance of paying attention.

Maybe tetherball is how our wars should be fought—with one country's representative on one side and the other country's representative on the other side. Then just blow the whistle and let the ball-hitting/face-slapping/cheek-stinging begin. One ruthless game of tetherball and no country would dare go to "war" again.

Now even tetherball has become an organized sport. And worse yet, did you know there are jacks and pick-up sticks tournaments now? There are even Twister competitions.

Is nothing sacred anymore?

Food eating has even become competitive. One guy in California recently broke the standing world record by eating fifty-nine hot dogs in twelve minutes. Who are the sponsors for a sport like this? Tums and Rolaids?

I'm fine with the NFL, the AFL, the NBA and most of the other sports organizations. I'm even okay with Little League and Pop Warner football. All I'm saying is leave some unorganized sports unorganized. Let's give the future generation the freedom to simply pick up a ball and toss it around a bit, without worrying about whether a talent scout is watching them.

They might discover something better than a trophy, a ring or a world championship. They might discover a healthy sense of fun.

Recapturing the Wonder

ONE AFTERNOON not long ago I sat on the front porch of my son's home watching my then-six-year-old granddaughter chase a grasshopper around the yard with a pink butterfly net. When she finally captured her prize, she showed it off as though she had just discovered some rare new species.

Ah, that sense of wonder. Can you remember having it as a child?

Whatever happened to it? Did it leave us on the 1,346th day in a row that we sat in the middle of rush-hour traffic? Did it seep out of our souls while we were busy trying to figure out where the money was going to come from to pay this month's bills? Did we surrender it in the midst of a conflict, an unpleasant encounter with a difficult person, or whatever else happened in our life to encroach upon our peace? When did we lose our sense of wonder, where did it go, and is it too late to get it to return to us?

I remember the very first time I tasted a honeysuckle flower. I was amazed that such a powerfully sweet flavor was hidden in that tiny plant. I enjoyed it so much that it became my daily ritual on my way home from elementary school. I'd pick a few honeysuckle flowers growing wild in the dirt, and that would be my treat for the walk home. To me, it was better than chasing after the ice cream truck. (And it took a lot less energy.)

Even though I haven't tasted a honeysuckle flower in decades, to this day I can recall its flavor. And the wonder.

I remember the sense of wonder I felt every time I added a new rock to my rock collection.

The first time I saw the Grand Canyon, I had that sense of wonder. These days, we're usually in too much of a hurry to pull off the road and take another look at it. We drive by the natural wonder on our way to someplace else. We know the Grand Canyon is there. *It* hasn't gone anywhere.

No, but our sense of wonder has.

Remember when looking at a butterfly could make your day, or watching a worm on a leaf, or seeing a rainbow in the sky?

Remember spending all day looking for a four-leaf clover in the grass and not caring how late it got?

Remember camping out in your backyard and looking up at the stars to see how many constellations you could find?

Remember the thrill of seeing a deer by the side of the road?

Remember the first time you walked through the gates of Disneyland?

Remember the first time you saw a waterfall?

Remember the first time you saw trees wearing their fall colors?

Remember going to the beach and bodysurfing in the waves?

Remember when you first learned to ride a bike?

Remember getting that one Christmas present you had wanted so desperately?

We've lost so much in our hurried society. We take so much for granted. The Seven Wonders of the World aren't the only places or experiences worthy of our awe. The world—and life—is full of them.

Whatever it takes, regain your sense of wonder.

Close, but Not Yet . . .

WE ALL HAVE OUR OWN brushes with death. As I've already
mentioned, mine started early—a serious car accident at three
months of age. Barely three months later, I was in one of
the deadliest tornados to ever hit Arkansas. (No wonder I'm a
little jumpy.)

The tornado was an F-4 and it killed forty-four people in the
nearby town of Judsonia alone. Then it moved through the edge of
our town, continuing its path of destruction.

The tornado hit in the late afternoon when my mother and
father were still at work. The lady who was watching us noticed
that the sky was looking ominous and decided she had better head
to her house to take care of her own family. After all, our parents
would be arriving home at any moment. With five kids, ten and
under, to care for, she had probably already survived a couple of
tornados that day and didn't want to deal with another one.

Unbeknownst to any of us, though, our parents were having
trouble making it home because of the storm.

With the wind howling and the hail beating down on the house,
my brother got us on the ground and then laid his body over us
while the storm passed.

Once it was safe, people started coming out of their homes to assess the damage. Some roofs had been blown off and trees uprooted near us, but the towns of nearby Judsonia and Bald Knob had been pretty much destroyed. The only building in Judsonia that wasn't damaged was the United Methodist Church.

Only six months old and already I'd had two brushes with death. There have been others.

Once when I was in the hospital, a nurse came into my room and told me she needed to give me another dose of insulin. I was feeling weak and wondered if I needed the shot. But because she was the nurse and I was the patient, I hesitated about saying anything.

But something inside of me wouldn't let it go. I knew I was having a low blood-sugar reaction. As she moved the needle toward my arm, I finally had the courage (read: "brains") to speak up. I told her how I was feeling and asked if she would test my blood before giving me the additional medication. She insisted I needed the medication but finally agreed to my request.

When the results of the blood test came back from the lab, that nurse and several others rushed into my hospital room with a large glass of orange juice. My blood sugar was in the twenties. That's about one-fifth what it should have been.

Later that evening, the night nurse came into my room and told me that giving me that shot probably would have killed me. I'm glad I spoke up.

During my lifetime I've survived two major California earthquakes—the 6.2 Sylmar quake and the 6.6 Northridge quake. And I've had other experiences where, had one thing gone differently—had I been two seconds earlier crossing that intersection, had I turned right instead of left—I might not be here today.

I'm sure you have plenty of your own stories. Some of your tales would probably top mine. If you get to this point in life, chances are you've cheated death a time or two.

I like to think one of the reasons we're still here is that we have more to do. Something else needs to be done, and the assignment has our name written on it.

In other words, God isn't through with us yet.

I Miss Handwritten Letters

HAVE YOU NOTICED that hardly anyone writes letters anymore? Oh, once in a while one arrives in your mailbox. But for the most part, letter writing is becoming obsolete. Sad, isn't it?

There's something about a handwritten letter that all the e-mail in cyberspace cannot replace. A letter feels different than an e-mail. An e-mail is fine for short, sweet messages. But when someone takes the time to sit down and write you a personal, handwritten letter these days, it's something to be noted and cherished.

I still have just about every letter my husband wrote me while we were dating. He has the letters I wrote to him too. We're both "letter historians." These letters are a document of our lives during those years—how we met, how we first fell in love, every date we went on.

Letters can tell you a lot. In fact, some historians read old letters and journals with almost as much interest as history books. Assuming the letters and journals are true in their content, these missives can give you a good look at someone's life at a designated period.

I used to love writing letters, but these days, I've become used to e-mail brevity.

Sharing your innermost feelings is not easy in an e-mail. For one thing, the other person's Delete button is far too accessible. Who wants to pour out her heart and then, in one split second, have it erased?

I feel sorry for couples today. They're trying to form lifelong relationships in two-sentence exchanges on some social networking site or by texting quick four- or five-word replies to each other. It's not the same as a romantic letter on perfumed stationery.

Handwritten letters have become so rare now that when I do receive one in the mail, I look at it differently. I appreciate the time the sender took to sit down and write it. I handle that letter far more carefully than I do my credit card statements. I don't use a handwritten letter as a coaster for my coffee cup.

I'll more than likely save it too. I have letters I've saved from my father, my mother and my grandmother, and I have just about every crayon-scribbled letter from my children and grandchildren. I keep favorite letters from friends and family. They mean a great deal to me.

I understand President Ronald Reagan was a great letter-writer. His love letters to his wife Nancy were put into a book, and my husband gave me a copy of it for our anniversary one year. It's a wonderful, romantic read.

With postage still less than half a buck, mailing a personal, handwritten letter to loved ones is a bargain. All you need is a pen and some paper, and a whole lot of heart.

Frost Warning

WE HEAR A LOT about how our weather is changing. But that's not the only thing that's getting colder on our planet. Some recent news stories reveal a good amount of frost has been seeping into people, as well.

Case in point: A Florida man was recently arrested for allegedly throwing a three-foot Christmas tree at his dad's head. When he missed, he prepared to take better aim with the metal tree stand. I don't know what the argument was about, but I don't think the line "Then I whacked Dad on the noggin with a Christmas tree" appears anywhere in the "Twas the Night Before Christmas" poem.

In Missoula, Montana, a college kid allegedly sneaked up behind a mall Santa and surprised him by smashing a pie in his face, saying, "What do you think of that, Santa?" (And Rudolph thought he was the only North Pole resident who's had to put up with ridicule.)

Even Santa himself has shown some anger issues on occasion. One Santa was arrested for allegedly beating a seventy-four-year-old woman with a two-by-four. Why? Because, according to him, he thought she was stealing from him.

In Sacramento, California, a man crashed his neighbor's Christmas party and allegedly started flashing a knife around. One of the partygoers decided to fight back by grabbing a candy cane out of the yard and beating the Scrooge out of the man. (Apparently, the knife-wielding man didn't get the memo on the proper way to RSVP to a holiday party.)

The news recently reported another frosty incident—this one involved a nineteen-year-old singer who allegedly stabbed another member of her metal band for "playing badly." Probably not the constructive criticism the band member was looking for.

Then there was the report of a patient at a New York psychiatric ward ER room who, after waiting there almost a full twenty-four hours, collapsed onto the floor, only to be ignored by everyone in the room, including some of the hospital staff. Sadly, the patient died.

Throw in the Walmart security guard who was trampled to death by shoppers eager to get a bargain, and two teenage girls in Minnesota who were allegedly abusing Alzheimer's patients at the nursing home where they worked, and it leaves you scratching your head as to what this world is coming to. We've even had a shoe thrown at one of our presidents abroad.

In the midst of all this negative news, though, we also heard the report of a woman in Tennessee who happily returned $100,000 in cash that she found in the restroom of a Cracker Barrel Restaurant. (See what an order of blueberry pancakes will do for your disposition?)

And did you hear the news story of a dog saving another dog who had been hit by a car as they both tried to cross a busy highway? The heroic dog used his teeth to drag his friend through oncoming traffic to safety. What a visual of true friendship! When do you need your friends most? When they're at your side as you make it safely across the street, or when they refuse to leave your side when you're flat on your back unable to move?

Another news story tells of two puppies that followed a three-year-old boy as he wandered away from home, and then spent the night with him in freezing temperatures. The puppies instinctively snuggled up next to the youngster, using their own body heat to keep the boy alive. Proving once again that we can all learn a lot from a dog.

We can learn a lot from good ol' Southerners who eat at Cracker Barrel too.

And from faithful friends who don't say, "Hey, you're the one who crossed the street. Now, fend for yourself."

Whether global warming and changing weather patterns are real or not, one thing is certain—the world would be a better place if we all had a little more warmth in our hearts, and a lot less chill.

I Don't Care

I CARE ABOUT A LOT of things in life. I care about my family. I care about my work. I care about my friends, old and new. I care about my home, as in "home," not "house." I care about the pets I love and have loved. I care about people who are truly hurting. I care about babies and children who don't have a mother or father to love them. I care about learning-disabled people. I care about people who are rejected or overlooked. And I'm getting better at caring about myself.

There are things I don't care much about. I used to care about them. In fact, I used to care about them a lot. But when I finally admitted that my caring was a huge waste of precious time, I didn't care about them anymore. Here is what I don't care about any longer, and why.

- I don't care about the stresses of tomorrow. I'll be able to stress over each problem soon enough. Why waste today doing that?

- I don't care about age. It's only a number. Numbers are important when it comes to dairy-freshness dates. They're not important when it comes to birthdays. So what if you're an experienced birthday reveler. Good for you!

- I don't care about people who judge others with a wrecking ball and themselves with a powder puff. They leave their targets in a mangled heap, giving an incorrect impression that God's grace has a sliding scale. It doesn't. It's either available to us all, or we're all sunk. Not one of us measures up.

- I don't care about pettiness. People who deal in it squander your energy and draw your attention away from things that truly matter.

- I don't care about media feeding frenzies on whatever celebrities are the latest to mess up their lives. If they've made some poor decisions, why would we want to push them into making more?

- I don't care about someone's past. Their future is what matters.

With all the important things to care about in the world today, why do we waste so much time on all this other stuff? In other words, *who cares?*

I Miss My Parents

I MISS MY PARENTS. I think about them a lot. They left this world years ago, but I can bring them back at the speed of a memory.

My mother had a great sense of fun. She loved to surprise us with trips to Disneyland or Knott's Berry Farm. We would wake up on a Saturday morning and without any hint whatsoever, she would announce, "We're going to Disneyland."

Disneyland was my mother's favorite place to go. She didn't ride a lot of the rides, but watching us gave her great pleasure. She would ride the carousel. I remember her and my grandmother riding it. They were both impressively mobile, even into their later years.

Living in Southern California, my mother would also take us to the beach, but that was a different experience altogether. She always wore a dress and carried her anvil-like purse with her as she walked across the sand.

I loved playing in the water or making castles in the sand. The only problem was we'd just get started and Mom would say, "Okay, let's go." We had barely gotten wet, and already it was time to go. Now, before you think this was a kid simply wanting to spend more time at the beach and not wanting to go when her mother said it was time, let me assure you that was not the case. We had literally just arrived, and my mother would announce that it was too cold, too sandy, too windy, too wet, too whatever, and it was time to go.

Another one of her favorite things to do was to go to gospel quartet concerts. My parents would drive for miles to attend these events several times a year. I remember watching the Blackwood Brothers, the Speer Family, the Statesmen, the Stamps Quartet, the Jordanaires and all the other legendary quartets of that time as they brought down the house. It was electrifying. Rock concerts had nothing on a gospel quartet concert.

Later in his life, one of my father's favorite things was to read farm realty magazines. He always dreamed of moving back to Arkansas one day, where he and my mother grew up, met and married and where all their kids were born. We moved to California when I, the last of the brood, was around two years old.

Dad would spend hours searching through those magazines, circling the farms that looked promising. Then, when I would come over for a visit, which was almost every day, he would proudly show me which farms he liked.

Dad never did get to move back to a farm. He died without realizing that dream.

Another thing my dad enjoyed doing was finding shortcuts. No matter what the directions showed, Dad knew there was a shortcut to be found, and he wouldn't stop until he found it. I never understood this confidence until I moved to the South. In the South, there are dozens of ways to get to the same place. And no, they don't all go through Atlanta.

Much like my dad, my father's brothers and one sister had great senses of humor. I remember my family coming home one night and entering the dark house. When we turned on the kitchen light, there on the kitchen table was a chair upon which sat a makeshift "body," dressed in my father's clothes. It startled us at first, but then my parents put two and two together and came up with one of my uncles. They were right; it turned out to be his handiwork, and they laughed over that prank for years.

My father had a history of pulling his own pranks, even as a boy. Such as when he maneuvered a cow into his schoolhouse and left it there so the teacher would discover it in the morning. Talk about a school's free milk program.

I miss my parents. I miss their laughter, their advice, their sense of fun, the way my mother would stand in front of the heater on a cold winter's day (yes, it does get cold in California). Most of all, I miss the doughnuts and cakes she would bring home on discount day at the old Helm's Bakery outlet. To her, glazed doughnuts were a food group.

Whenever we had a family dinner—which was about once a month (we'd celebrate whoever's birthday had taken place in that month) and that's not counting the holiday get-togethers—Mom was usually in charge of bringing the desserts. She would fill an entire table full of sweet goodies. Even if it wasn't anyone's birthday that month, we'd have several birthday cakes she had found on the discount rack at the local grocery store bakery.

"Who's Don?"

"Don?"

"The cake says 'Happy Birthday, Don.'"

"Oh. It was on sale. Look, it's chocolate."

Mom loved her sweets. She was surrounded by diabetics (we ended up with several in our immediate family), but she kept her weekly rendezvous with Helm's Bakery. Her sweet tooth had deep, deep roots.

I miss my father too. I remember seeing him weep in his hospital bed after he had a heart malfunction and doctors inserted a temporary pacemaker. He was concerned that he was coming to the end of his life, and he wondered if he was ready to go—a question nearly everyone ponders at some point in their life, I suppose. Luckily, he had plenty of time between that day and his last breath to answer that question for himself.

Parents bring us into this world, but for most of us, they don't see us out. As painful as it is, we usually have to watch them exit first. Nothing is easy about that. Nothing is easy about watching your mom and dad go from strong, healthy and seemingly invulnerable people to a mere whisper of their former selves. And, despite the months or years of degeneration that take place right before your eyes, it seems to happen overnight.

If your parents are no longer here, I'm sure you can identify with what I'm saying. Wouldn't it have been nice to have had them stay around a little longer? So much happens in our own later years that we would really like to discuss with them. All that advice they so freely gave us in our teenage years, when we were too busy to listen, would be so welcomed now, wouldn't it? I wonder what my parents would think about the shape the world is in today. I wonder if my mother would have enjoyed retirement, a retirement she never really was able to have. After working for most of her life, the only rest she got was when she was flat on her back, fighting cancer. That doesn't seem fair to me. But then, a lot that happens in life doesn't seem fair.

I know my parents would have been amazed at how many great-grandchildren they have now. They would have loved the fact that there are a set of twins among them.

And my mom would still be bringing birthday cakes home from the bakery.

I was just beginning to take my mother away on trips, such as to Washington, DC, a city she had always wanted to visit. She was too busy with work and other commitments before, but finally she started letting me take her on trips and she was enjoying getting away. I wonder where else we might have gone.

I wonder if my dad would have ever bought his farm.

I wonder if my mom would have ever learned to put her needs first.

I miss my parents.

Enough Is Enough

GROWING UP, you could easily tell when your mother or father had had enough. A certain look, a click of the tongue, a snap of the finger or a narrowing of the eyes signaled *enough was enough.*

We don't always know when enough is enough at an all-you-can-eat buffet. But at least most of us put the fork down before the restaurant has to remove their double doors so we can exit the building. Just in time, we say "Enough is enough."

Most of us have reached a place where we're saying enough is enough to credit cards. With the ridiculously high interest rates and unreasonable fees they keep charging us, credit accounts are being closed all over America. Why? Because enough is enough.

Our instincts usually tell us when enough is enough when we're dealing with a bully. We may put up with one for weeks, months, even years, but there finally comes that moment when we've had it, and at long last we draw a healthy boundary. Enough is enough.

We have a harder time figuring out, though, when "enough is enough" when it comes to our wants . . . uh, I mean our *needs.* It's easy to mix those two up. After a lifetime of moving from house to better house and buying cars, toys, jewelry and whatever else we happen to collect, when will we finally be ready to say *Enough is enough?* When will we utter those words, "I can't think of another thing that I want . . . er, . . . I mean, need." When will we be full, satisfied, complete and happy?

When will enough be enough?

I have things in my house that I don't need, haven't used, and don't even like, but at some point in my life, I was convinced that I had to have them.

I didn't need them. In fact, I probably have enough stuff to last me the rest of my life.

There, I've said it. Enough is enough. I have enough. I could switch things around a bit—buy a different house or a different car. I could even buy a new outfit or two. But I don't *need* them. My closet certainly isn't full, but what's in there would take me years to wear out. My house is fine. My car is too. I have enough. You probably do too. Not that we can't work for more, but we have enough.

And enough is enough. It truly is.

Ten Things

CHANCES ARE YOU'VE HEARD about the popular book, *1000 Places To See before You Die*. Although I'm sure they're all wonderful points of interest, here is my own list of just ten important things I hope you get to see before you die.

Ten Things To See before You Die

1. Your backyard.

Are you paying for land you never walk on or look at or whose existence you don't even acknowledge other than that one hour a week when you mow it? Have you ever gone on a day's outing in your backyard? Had a picnic there? Strolled the grounds? Picked some flowers?

We see our front yard every day when we drive up the driveway and then get out of our car and walk by it. We notice it long before it needs mowing or the hedge needs trimming back. Some days we even cross over it on our way out to our mailbox, or when we look through the bushes (or on our roof) for the morning paper.

But our backyard is a different story. We know it's there. No one's moved it, we're quite certain of that. But when's the last time we spent an afternoon sitting out there enjoying the arbor we built ten years ago or relaxing in the shade of the trees we planted when our children were young?

Before you die, I hope you get to see your backyard and make a lot more memories.

2. Your dining room table.

In the hustle-bustle of what was our young adult life, our dining room tables may not have had much use. With fast food far too available, and everyone's schedule way too busy, the family dining room table can be one of the least used pieces of furniture in a house.

When I was growing up, we always sat at the dining room table for dinner. It was where conversations happened. You can't have a conversation when one person eats dinner in the recliner, watching television, and the other person eats on a stool in the kitchen.

I hope that before you die, you get to enjoy your dining room table. And each other's undistracted company. I hope your dining room table can never be sold as "barely used."

3. Your family.

Before you die, I hope you get to see your family. Really see them. Not as a blur on your way out the door. Or a meal shared, a hug on their birthday, or a phone call when some crisis needs to be handled. I hope you take in all there is to see and experience—their laughter, their hopes, their questions, their pain and their love. I hope you share as much of yourself with them as you can spare. I hope they know you and you know them. I hope before you die, you've left a lot of souvenirs in their hearts to remember you by.

4. Your pew.

Before you die, I hope you get to spend time in your pew. Faith is an important part of life. When times are tough, it will be your faith that will get you through them.

If your pew is a distant memory, or if you've never sat in one (and a pew can be in your heart too), I recommend you put that on your must-see list. The view of your life from the vantage point of faith can change your whole perspective.

5. Your smile.

If you've lost your smile over the years, I hope that before you die, you find it again. It's still there. It might not be easy for it to crack through the years of disappointments, hurt, loss and sorrow. But if you keep trying, your smile will eventually shine through. I hope you let it. People around you would surely benefit from seeing it again. Life's too short to lose your smile.

6. Old friends.

If there are old friends who cross your mind every now and then, and you wonder how they're doing, I hope before you die, you reconnect with them. They just might be wondering how you're doing too.

Old friends, the ones who have stood the test of time, who walked with you through the rain instead of leaving and then reappearing when the sun came back out, are the eighth wonder of the world. These kinds of friends are rare, and to be cherished.

If you've lost touch through the busyness of life, take the time to call them up. Or write them a letter. Let them know how much their presence in your life has meant to you over the years.

Before you die, I hope you visit lots of old friends.

7. Your dreams.

Too many dreams die with the person they've been given to. What were your dreams? Have you fulfilled them yet? Have you told yourself it's too late?

I hope that before you die, you take a few more steps to pursue those dreams that were put inside of you. There are plenty of testimonies of people who didn't start their dream career until middle age and beyond. I've highlighted a few in this book. There are countless others.

Don't miss out on the scenery in the second half of your life. Don't give up on your dreams.

8. Yourself.

Do you know you? Have you ever gotten to know, *really know* the one person you spend the most time with? Have you shown yourself the same respect you've shown to others when it came to their opinions, their complaints, and their dreams? Have you cut yourself slack when you've made mistakes, or do you only overlook the mistakes of others? Do you give yourself second, third and fourth chances, or did you give up on yourself after the first one?

Before you die, I hope you spend time visiting yourself. You don't have to talk out loud to yourself (or, at least, if you do, stick an earpiece in your ear so people will think you're on your cell phone). But time spent getting to know *you* is never wasted.

And who better to be an expert on you than *you?*

9. Your hometown.

Sometime before you leave this world, take a trip to your hometown. Revisit your school, the house where you grew up, the corner store where you bought your sodas, the movie theater where you watched all the old classics. You'll be amazed at how much and how little difference there is. Buildings, if they're even still standing, will look so much smaller than you remember them. You'll see the areas that succumbed to progress and the areas that haven't changed a bit. You might even run into that bully who used to give you so much trouble. Who knows? He might be the mayor now.

In most situations—not all, but in most—it's good to go back. It's good to take another look at a place where your personality was molded. A place where you first laughed, first cried and first discovered that you had it within yourself to survive whatever life might throw at you. The simple fact that you're holding this book in your hands is proof that you were correct in your assessment—you have survived what life has handed to you. And you're no doubt stronger for it.

I hope before you die, you visit the place of your childhood and get reacquainted with the kid you were back then. You just might become the best of friends.

10. Your life.

This is the big one. It's not the pyramids, the Eiffel Tower, an African safari or a Hawaiian cruise. It's even more amazing. Yet so many people die without ever getting to see it. What is it? It's their life.

Before you pack it all up and leave this world, I hope you take the time to experience your life. I hope you're fully present for each and every moment. I hope you write journals, take lots of pictures, write lots of letters, make lots of phone calls to friends, enjoy time with your children, cherish time with your spouse, take in all there is to see, share your stories, use every one of your God-given talents to the fullest, learn new skills, become the best person you're capable of becoming, and don't let a day, an hour or a minute slip away from you without being aware that it's going. Don't be one of those people who looks back over his or her life and wonders where all the years went. See, feel, live your life. It's the greatest wonder of the world.

Other Books by Martha Bolton

Didn't My Skin Used to Fit?

Cooking with Hot Flashes

Your Best Nap Now

I Think, Therefore I Have a Headache!

Race You to the Fountain of Youth

It's Always Darkest before the Fridge Door Opens

Growing Your Own Turtleneck . . . and Other Benefits of Aging